※

Sociology as a Life or Death Issue

Robert J. Brym
University of Toronto

WADSWORTH
CENGAGE Learning™

Australia • Brazil • Japan • Korea • Mexico • Singapore • Spain • United Kingdom • United States

WADSWORTH
CENGAGE Learning™

Sociology as a Life or Death Issue, First Edition

Robert J. Brym

Acquisitions Editor: Chris Caldeira

Assistant Editor: Melanie Cregger

Editorial Assistant: Rebecca Boorsma

Technology Project Manager: Lauren Keyes

Marketing Manager: Meghan Pease

Marketing Assistant: Ileana Shevlin

Marketing Communications Manager: Tami Strang

Project Manager, Editorial Production: Cheri Palmer

Creative Director: Rob Hugel

Art Director: Caryl Gorska

Print Buyer: Paula Vang

Permissions Editor: Mardell Schultz

Production Service: Matrix Productions Inc.

Illustrator: Graphic World

Cover Designer: Riezebos Holzbaur Design Group

Cover Image: Jason Reed/ Corbis

Compositor: International Typesetting and Composition

For product information and technology assistance, contact us at **Cengage Learning Customer & Sales Support, 1-800-354-9706**

For permission to use material from this text or product, submit all requests online at **cengage.com/permissions**
Further permissions questions can be e-mailed to **permissionrequest@cengage.com**

Library of Congress Control Number: 2008925825

ISBN-13: 978-0-495-60075-6

ISBN-10: 0-495-60075-X

Wadsworth
10 Davis Drive
Belmont, CA 94002-3098
USA

Cengage Learning is a leading provider of customized learning solutions with office locations around the globe, including Singapore, the United Kingdom, Australia, Mexico, Brazil, and Japan. Locate your local office at **international.cengage.com/region**

Cengage Learning products are represented in Canada by Nelson Education, Ltd.

For your course and learning solutions, visit **academic.cengage.com**

Purchase any of our products at your local college store or at our preferred online store, **www.ichapters.com**

Printed in Canada
1 2 3 4 5 6 7 12 11 10 09 08

In memory of my mother
Sophie Brym (1912–2004)

שפרה מרים ברים, אשת-חיל

ז"ל

✷

Contents

List of Figures and Tables

FIGURES

v

TABLES

✳

Preface

We say an object is three-dimensional if it possesses length, width, and depth. It resides in the fourth dimension—time—if it exists for more than an instant. People usually experience the four dimensions effortlessly. You don't have to think much to know that you're holding a book in your hands and that time is passing as you read it, and most 14-year-old boys don't have to try hard to find the sleek shape of a shiny pair of Nike Zoom Kobe III basketball shoes pleasing and know they are brand new.

In contrast, you need training to see the fifth dimension. Is it worth the effort? I invite you to read the next hundred or so pages and judge for yourself. I argue that the benefits are enormous. Seeing in five dimensions helps people live longer and fuller lives.

The fifth dimension is the *social*. Those new Nike Zoom Kobe IIIs, which sell for $130, cost about $7 to make in a crowded and poorly ventilated Indonesian factory. While Kobe Bryant and major Nike shareholders get rich selling them, the 16-year-old girl who makes them works 15 hours a day for 20 cents an hour. Some college students find this situation deplorable and have organized an anti-Nike campaign and boycott to fight against it. Other college students note that the young factory worker probably prefers her job to the alternative—taking care of her siblings and the family goat back in her village for no pay and no prospects at all—and that she is helping her poor country industri-alize. From their point of view, buying Nike Zoom Kobe IIIs benefits everyone. Boycott or buy? Seen from the fifth (social) dimension, an entire world of human relations and a moral dilemma are embedded in those basketball shoes. And what is true for Nike Zoom Kobe IIIs is true for everything else in your life. Like it or not, you are part of soci-ety, and your actions, no matter how personal they appear, have conse-quences for others. It follows that if you want people to enjoy longer, richer lives, you need to make informed decisions about Nike Zoom Kobe IIIs—and everything else you see before you.

That's where sociology comes in. **Sociology** is the systematic study of human behavior in social context. Sociologists analyze the social relations that lie beneath ordinary aspects of everyday life—everything from basketball shoes to homelessness, fame to racial dis-crimination, sex to religious zeal.

At its best, sociology speaks to the big issues of the day and the big issues of life, and it speaks to a broad audience. Accordingly, my aim in writing this little book was to speak plainly about the urgent need to think sociologically. Sociological understanding, I argue, is a life-or-death issue. I don't make that claim for dramatic effect. I mean it lit-erally. By helping us understand the social causes of death, sociology can help us figure out how to live better. Hence the urgency of socio-logical knowledge.

I develop my argument in five linked essays. In the title essay I argue that it is useful to keep in mind the inevitability of death because doing so compels us to focus on how to live best in our remaining time. I then outline how higher education in general and the sociological perspective in particular can contribute to that goal.

The next three chapters add substance to the assertions of the opening essay. I examine death due to violence and death due to sup-posedly natural disasters and find that in both cases powerful social forces help to determine who lives and who dies. To make my case, I enter three worlds that figure prominently in popular culture and the evening news—those of American hip hop, Palestinian suicide bombers, and the victims of hurricanes in the Caribbean region and the coast of the Gulf of Mexico.

Hip hop arose in desperate social circumstances and was originally a protest against them. However, its message got diluted as the music became commercialized, and now it misguides many young people about how to best live their lives. A sociological understanding of hip hop holds out hope for correcting the problem.

Many Westerners think that suicide bombings are conducted by crazed religious zealots and that the appropriate response to them is overwhelming military force. My sociological analysis of Palestinian suicide bombing against Israelis shows that this way of thinking is flawed. The conflict between Palestinians and Israelis has deep political and emotional roots. Responding to suicide bombing with overwhelming military force only worsens the conflict and causes more deaths on both sides. Sociological analysis suggests an alternative approach.

When Hurricane Katrina killed about 2,300 Americans in 2005, some people said the deaths were an awful consequence of a rare natural disaster while others said they could have been avoided if the president weren't a racist. Sociologically speaking, these judgments are hopelessly naïve. They do nothing to help us understand how disasters like Katrina can be prevented in the future. In contrast, my sociological analysis shows that patterns of class and racial inequality were responsible for most Katrina-related deaths and that other societies with different patterns of class and racial inequality have been more successful than the United States in avoiding such catastrophes. Again, sociology points the way to avoiding death and improving life.

Many students just beginning college want to know what sociology is and what they can do with a sociology degree. In the concluding essay, I draw on material from the preceding chapters to sketch the broad outlines of the discipline and offer career advice to undergraduates. I argue that my analyses of the social causes of death illustrate the fundamental aim of sociology at its best. Learning about the fifth dimension allows us to extend the third and fourth dimensions, helping us deepen and prolong life.

ACKNOWLEDGMENTS

Authors often say that they alone bear responsibility for their work. For two reasons, I make no such claim here.

First, I am a sociologist, and I therefore delight in acknowledging that I am embedded in intellectual and publishing networks whose members have helped to shape my work. I gladly share with them a full measure of responsibility for this book's strengths and weaknesses. Among the co-owners of this volume are colleagues who read and offered critical comments on all or part of the manuscript and provided useful bibliographic assistance: Bader Araj, Shyon Baumann, John Kirk, Rhonda Lenton, Adie Nelson, Jack Veugelers, and Malcolm Mackinnon. I would also like to thank the following reviewers: Tim Delaney, SUNY Oswego; Casey Cornelius, Delta College; Sue Wika, Minnesota State Community & Technical College; Yasemin Basen-Cassino, Montclair State; Jean Lynch-Brandon, Lansing Community College; Scott Potter, Marion Technical College; and Russell Willis, Grambling State University. Also culpable are the members of the editorial, marketing, and production team at Wadsworth, who saw the value of my initial proposal and offered much encouragement and useful critical advice: Chris Caldeira, Cheri Palmer, Erin Parkins, and Melanie Cregger. I hope you all feel that the final product justifies your deeply appreciated efforts.

A journalist once asked the great Jewish poet, Chaim Nachman Bialik (1873–1934), whether he preferred speaking Hebrew or Yiddish. Bialik answered in Yiddish: "*Hebraish ret man; Yiddish ret sikh*" ("Hebrew one speaks; Yiddish speaks by itself.") I understand what he meant. Like all authors, I have struggled mightily on many occasions to get things right. This time, however, the job was almost effortless. That is the second reason I don't claim sole responsibility for this book: it practically wrote itself.

About the Author

Robert J. Brym (www.chass.utoronto
.ca/brym) is Professor of Sociology at the
University of Toronto and the 2007 winner
of the Northrop Frye Award, given annually to a faculty member for innovation in
teaching and conveying the importance
of research to students. He has published
widely on politics and society in Russia,
Canada, and the Middle East and is currently
researching collective violence in Israel, the
West Bank, and Gaza. Bob's popular in-
troductory sociology textbook, *Sociology: Your Compass for a New World*
(with John Lie), has appeared in American, Canadian, Brazilian, and
Australian editions; the American edition is published by Wadsworth.
Bob began teaching introductory sociology immediately after graduate
school and can't stop.

© Greg Dean/Signature Studios

1

Sociology as a Life or Death Issue[1]

A DETOUR

To inspire you, I will take the unusual course of talking about death. I apologize in advance if this makes you uncomfortable. I know it is customary when addressing undergraduates to remind them that they are young, have accomplished much, and are now in a position to make important decisions that will shape the rest of their lives. I will eventually get around to that too. But to arrive at the optimistic and uplifting part I feel I must take a detour through the valley of the shadow of death.

When I was 7 years old, I lived across the street from a park where I engaged in all the usual childhood games with my friends. We played tag, hide-and-seek, baseball, and cops-and-robbers. We also invented a game that we awkwardly called "See Who Drops Dead the Best." We would line ourselves up on a park bench and choose one boy to shoot

---

1 This is an expanded version of a commencement address delivered in May 2005 to graduates of the "Steps to University" Program, University of Toronto. "Steps to University" identifies promising high school students who might otherwise not complete school or attend college because of their economic and social circumstances and offers them selected university courses to encourage them to pursue postsecondary education.

the rest of us in turn, using a tree branch as a machine gun. Once shot, we did our best to scream, fall to the ground, writhe, convulse, and expire. The shooter would choose the most convincing victim—the boy who dropped dead the best—to play shooter in the next round. The game would occupy us for ten minutes or so, after which we'd pick ourselves up and move on to baseball. At the age of 7, death was entertaining.

I didn't live in a war zone and there were no deaths in my family, so I really didn't begin to take death personally until I was 15. Then, one Sunday evening, it suddenly dawned on me that someday I would *really* die, losing consciousness forever. The moment this realization hit, I ran to my parents in panic. I rudely switched off the TV and asked them to tell me immediately why we were living if we were going to die anyway. My parents looked at each other, stunned, and then smiled nervously, perhaps thinking their son had taken leave of his senses. They were not especially religious people, and they had only a few years of elementary schooling between them. They had no idea how to address questions about the meaning of life. Eventually my father confessed he didn't know the answer to my question, whereupon I ran to my bedroom, shouting that my parents were fools to have lived half a century without even knowing why they were alive. From that moment and for the next three decades, death became a source of anxiety for me.

DENIAL

And so it is for most adolescents and adults. We all know that we might die at any moment. This knowledge makes most of us anxious. Typically, we react to our anxiety by denying death. To a degree, denying death helps us to calm ourselves.

The denial of death takes many forms. One is religious. Religion offers us immortality, the promise of better times to come, and the security of benevolent spirits who look over us. It provides meaning and purpose in a world that might otherwise seem cruel and senseless (James, 1976: 123, 139).

In one of its extreme forms, religion becomes what philosophers call **determinism,** the belief that everything happens the way it does because it was destined to happen in just that way. From the determinist's viewpoint, we can't really choose how to live because forces larger than us control life. Even religions that say we can choose between good and evil are somewhat deterministic because they guarantee eternal life only if we choose to do good, and that requires submitting to the will of God as defined by some authority, not us. Many people worry less about death because they believe that the reward for submitting to the will of God is eternal life in heaven.[2]

A second way in which we calm our anxiety about death involves trying to stay young. Consider the cosmetic surgery craze. Every week, millions of North Americans watch *Nip/Tuck, The Swan, Extreme Makeover,* and other popular TV series about cosmetic surgery. Every year, millions of North Americans undergo cosmetic and reconstructive surgical procedures (including dermabrasion and Botox injections). In 2005 alone, 10.5 million plastic surgeries were performed in North America, up nearly 2,500 percent since 1992, when statistics were first collected (American Society of Plastic Surgeons, 2006). And that's not all we do to stay young. We diet. We exercise. We take vitamin supplements. We wear make-up. We dye our hair. We strive for stylishness in our dress. We celebrate youthfulness and vitality in movies, music, and advertising. We even devalue the elderly and keep them segregated in nursing homes and hospitals, in part so we won't be constantly reminded of our own mortality.

The search for eternal youth is a form of what philosophers call **voluntarism,** the belief that we alone control our destiny. From the voluntarist's point of view, we can overcome forces larger than us and thereby make whatever we want of our lives. Thus, many people worry less about death because they delude themselves into thinking they can cheat it.

---

2 Secular versions of determinism also exist. Various forms of nationalism and communism promise a heavenly future for certain nations or classes. Paradoxically, however, they require that individuals submit to a higher party or state authority and act in prescribed ways if they hope to achieve what is supposedly historically inevitable (Berlin, 2002a).

A TRAP

I have good news and bad news for you, and I'm going to deliver the bad news first. The bad news is that the denial of death is a trap. Denying death makes it more difficult to figure out how to live well and thus be happy.

Let's say, for example, that a religion promises you eternal life in exchange for obeying certain rules. One rule says you can marry people only of your own religion. Another says that once you marry you can't divorce. A third severely limits the steps you can take to control the number of children you have. A fourth says you have to marry someone of the opposite sex. Many people live comfortably by these rules, but the same rules make other people miserable. That, however, is the price they must pay for the religion's promise of eternal life. In general, by denying people the opportunity to figure out and do what is best for them as individuals, the deterministic denial of death can make some people deeply unhappy.

So can the voluntaristic denial of death. In the TV series *Nip/Tuck,* plastic surgeons Christian Troy and Sean McNamara begin each consultation with these words: "Tell me what you don't like about yourself." Notice that they don't ask prospective patients what they dislike about their bodies. They ask them what they dislike about their *selves.* They assume that your body faithfully represents your self—that your weight, proportions, color, scars, and hairiness say something fundamentally important about your character, about who you are. If, however, we believe our happiness depends on our physical perfection and youthfulness, we are bound to be unhappy because nobody can be perfect and because we will inevitably grow old and die. And in the meantime, pursuing youthfulness in the belief that you are no more than your appearance distracts you from probing deeply and finding out who you really are and what you need from life to make you happy. I conclude that denying death for whatever reason prevents you from figuring out how to live in the way that is best for you.[3]

---

3 Some scientists believe we will conquer death before this century is over by developing the ability to upload our minds to robots (Kurzweil, 1999). If that happens, I may have plenty of time to revise my argument accordingly.

HIGHER EDUCATION

Finally, some good news: You don't have to deny death and thus become distracted from figuring out what you need to do to live a happy life. Instead, you can try to remain aware that you will die and that you could die at any moment. That awareness will inevitably cause you to focus on how best to achieve a meaningful life in your remaining time: the kind of career you need to pursue to make you happiest, the kind of person with whom you need to develop a long-term intimate relationship, the way you can best contribute to the welfare of others, the political principles you should follow, and so on. As an old saying goes, the gallows in the morning focuses the mind wonderfully (Frankl, 1959).

I have more good news. People are well equipped to figure out how best to live. That is because we are meaning-creating machines. Faced with ambiguity in any social setting, we instantly start investing imaginative energy to define the situation and figure out what is expected of us and others. We abhor uncertainty, so we always strive to make social reality meaningful (Berger and Luckmann, 1967). And since there is nothing more uncertain or ambiguous than death, when we face awareness of our own mortality we almost instinctively want to create a durable purpose for our lives (Becker, 1971, 1973). In fact, we are so devoted to making life meaningful that we have created an institution especially devoted to helping us discover what the good life is for each of us: the system of higher education.

I imagine your parents and teachers have told you to stay in school as long as you can because a degree is a ticket to a good job. They are right, at least in part. A stack of studies shows that each additional year of education will increase your annual income for the rest of your life. Moreover, the economic value of education increases year after year (Appleby, Fougère, and Rouleau, 2004). But the view that colleges and universities are just places for job training is a half truth. Above all, the system of higher education was developed as a place devoted to the discovery, by rational means, of truth, beauty, and the good life. Said differently, if you treat higher education not just as job training but as a voyage of self-discovery, you will increase your chance of finding out what you value in life, what you can achieve, and how you can achieve it.

Colleges and universities are divided into different departments, centers, schools, and faculties, each with a different approach to improving the welfare of humanity. The physician heals; the instructor in physical education teaches how to improve strength, stamina, and vigor; and the philosopher demonstrates the value of living an examined life. A good undergraduate education will expose you to many different approaches to improving your welfare and that of humanity as a whole and will give you a chance to discover which of them suits you.

What does the sociological approach offer?

SOCIOLOGY

The sociological approach to improving human welfare is based on the idea that the social relations we have with other people create opportunities for us to think and act but also set limits on our thoughts and actions. Accordingly, we can better understand what we are and what we can become by studying the social relations that help shape us.

A classic illustration of the sociological approach to understanding the world and improving human welfare is Émile Durkheim's late-nineteenth-century study of suicide in France (Durkheim, 1951 [1897]; Hamlin and Brym, 2006). Most people think that suicide is the most nonsocial and antisocial action imaginable, a result of deep psychological distress that is typically committed in private and involves a rejection of society and everything it stands for. Yet Durkheim showed that high rates of psychological distress often do not result in a high suicide rate while low rates of psychological distress sometimes do. He also argued that the rate and type of suicide that predominates in a society tells us something fundamentally important about the state of that society as a whole.[4]

---

4 Dividing the number of times an event occurs (e.g., the number of suicides in a certain place and period) by the total number of people to whom the event could occur in principle (e.g., the number of people in that place and period) and then calculating how many times it would occur in a population of standard size (e.g., 100,000) will give you the **rate** at which an event occurs. Rates let you compare groups of different size. For instance, if 2 suicides occur in a town of 10,000 people and 4 suicides occur in a city of 100,000 people, the suicide rate is 20 per 100,000 in the town and 4 per 100,000 in the city.

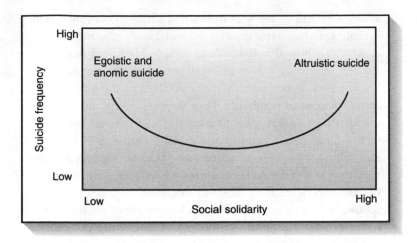

FIGURE 1.1 Durkheim's Theory of Suicide

Note: Durkheim argued that as the level of social solidarity increases, the suicide rate declines. Then, beyond a certain point, it starts to rise. Hence the U-shaped curve in this graph. Durkheim called suicides that occur in high-solidarity settings **altruistic suicides**. In contrast, suicide that occurs in low-solidarity settings is egoistic or anomic, said Durkheim. **Egoistic suicide** results from a lack of integration of the individual into society because of weak social ties to others. **Anomic suicide** occurs when norms governing behavior become vaguely defined.

According to Durkheim, the probability that your state of mind will lead you to commit suicide is influenced by the social relations in which you are embedded—in particular, the frequency with which you interact with others and the degree to which you share their beliefs, values, and moral standards. Durkheim referred to the frequency of interaction and the degree of sharing of beliefs, values, and morals in a group as its level of **social solidarity.**

Simplifying for brevity's sake, Durkheim analyzed the effects of three levels of social solidarity on suicide rates (for details, see the note accompanying Figure 1.1):

■ *Low solidarity:* According to Durkheim, groups and societies characterized by a low level of social solidarity typically have a high suicide rate. Interacting infrequently and sharing few beliefs, values, and moral standards, people in low-solidarity settings lack emotional support and cultural guidelines for behavior. They are therefore more prone to commit suicide if they experience distress. Accordingly, Durkheim found that married adults were half as likely as unmarried adults to commit suicide because marriage typically created social ties and a moral cement that bound individuals to society. He found that women were only a third as likely as men to commit suicide because they were generally more involved in the intimate social relations of family life. Jews were less likely to commit suicide than Christians because centuries of persecution had turned them into a group that was more defensive and tightly knit. Elderly people were more prone than young and middle-aged people to take their own lives when faced with misfortune because they were most likely to live alone, to have lost a spouse, and to lack a job and a wide network of friends. On a broader, historical canvas, Durkheim viewed rising suicide rates as a symptom of the state of modern society. In general, social ties are weakening, he argued, and people share fewer beliefs, values, and moral standards than they used to.

- *Intermediate solidarity:* It follows that if we want suicide rates to decline, we must figure out ways of increasing the strength of social ties and shared culture in modern society. For example, if North Americans created a system of high-quality, universally accessible daycare, then more children would be better supervised, enjoy more interaction with peers and adults, and be exposed to similar socializing influences. At the same time, more adults (particularly single mothers) would be able to work in the paid labor force and form new social ties with their workmates. By thus raising the level of social solidarity, we would expect the suicide rate to drop.

- *High solidarity:* Despite a *general* decline in social solidarity, some groups are characterized by exceptionally high levels of social solidarity. When members of such a group perceive that the group is threatened, they are likely to be willing to sacrifice their lives to protect it. For instance, a soldier who is a member of a close-knit military unit may protect his buddies by throwing himself on a grenade that is about to explode. Similarly, some suicide bombers see the existence of their group threatened by a foreign power occupying their homeland. They are willing to give up their lives to coerce the occupying power into leaving (Pape, 2005). The increased rate of suicide bombing in the world since the early 1980s is in part a symptom of increasing threats posed to high-solidarity groups by foreign occupying forces. It follows that if we want fewer suicide bombings, one thing we can do is to figure out ways of ensuring that high-solidarity groups feel less threatened.

Much of the best sociological research today follows Durkheim's example. Sociologists frequently strive to identify (1) a type of behavior that for personal, political, or intellectual reasons they regard as interesting or important; (2) the specifically social forces—the patterns of social relations among people—that influence that behavior, and (3) the larger institutional, political, or other changes that might effectively improve human welfare with respect to the behavior of interest. By conducting research that identifies these three elements, sociologists help people understand what they are and what they can become in particular social and historical contexts (Mills, 1959).

WINNING THE GAME

You have accomplished much and are now in a position to make important decisions that will shape the rest of your life. At this threshold I challenge you not to be seduced by popular ways of denying death. I challenge you to remain aware that life is short and that by getting a higher education you will have the opportunity to figure out how to live in a way that will make you happiest. I personally hope you find sociology enlightening in this regard. But more important, you should know that higher education in general ought to encourage you to play the game of "See Who Lives Life the Best." You will be declared a winner if you play the game seriously. Socrates once said to his pupils that "What we are engaged in here isn't a chance conversation but a dialogue about the way we ought to live our lives." Accept nothing less from your professors.

CRITICAL THINKING EXERCISES

1. Make a list of the three most important goals you want to achieve in life. Beside each goal, write a sentence describing how you hope to achieve it. Exchange your list with a classmate. Write three paragraphs about whether you think each of your classmate's goals are worthwhile and whether the means he or she specified for achieving them are realistic. Discuss your evaluation with your classmate. Write two paragraphs answering the following questions: What makes a life goal worthwhile? What makes a plan for achieving a life goal realistic?

2. List three sociological problems you would like to know more about. Write three paragraphs answering the following questions: What would you like to know about these sociological problems? Why are these problems important to you? How do you think you can find out more about them?

3. Durkheim discussed the association between the level of social solidarity and the likelihood of committing suicide. How do you think the level of social solidarity might influence the crime rate, the divorce rate, and a group's state of health? Why do you think social solidarity might have these effects? Write three paragraphs answering these questions.

2

❋

Hip Hop from Caps to Bling

STROLLING DOWN THE AVENUE

In January 2006, my wife and I were attending a conference in New York. One afternoon we decided to take a break and walk over to Central Park. The weather was unusually pleasant for the time of year, and we enjoyed people-watching and window-shopping until we reached the pricey stores on Fifth Avenue. There, a barricade manned by two of New York's finest stopped our progress. About 30 feet farther down the street a second barricade blocked pedestrian traffic flowing in the opposite direction. The barricades cleared a space in front of Salvatore Ferragamo's flagship store, famous for its thousand-dollar shoes, stylish handbags, and other must-have accessories for the well-to-do.

Two black Lincoln Navigators were parked in front of the store. A high-tech garden of antennas and satellite dishes sprouted from the roof of one of them. Its tinted windows were shut. The windows of the second Navigator were wide open, and we could clearly see the driver and three other men inside, all clad in black. The passengers held AK-47 assault rifles upright. They wanted us to notice them. Two tall, athletic-looking men in suits, white shirts, ties, and well-tailored overcoats stood on either side of the store's front door, their eyes roaming the crowd. Each had his right hand inside his overcoat, presumably gripping a firearm. About half a dozen police vans and cruisers were blocking vehicular traffic. Police officers stood outside their cruisers. Whatever emergency was in progress, an intimidating company of about two dozen well-armed men was positioned to deal with it.

"Hey!" I said to one of the men in blue. "Did you guys catch Osama or something?"

The police officer suppressed a smile. "Not yet," he replied.

"So what's up?" I persisted.

"Can't say."

"Aw, come on. You can't stop all these taxpayers from enjoying the nice weather without an explanation. What's the occasion?"

"I guess Puffy needs a new tie."

"You mean Diddy, the hip hop artist?"

"Whatever."

In hip hop slang, "caps" are bullets and "bling" is flashy jewelry, as in "You don' hand over dat bling, I'ma bust a cap in yo' ass." Caps are the means, bling is the goal, as in the title of 50 Cent's 2005 movie, "Get Rich or Die Tryin'." There was no slaughter on Fifth Avenue that fine January day, but I have to admit that, like the rest of the crowd, my wife and I were captivated by the staged threat of violence and the spectacle of material excess offered by Diddy's shopping excursion. We knew the show was contrived for publicity—Diddy is not the President of the United States, and Fifth Avenue is not the inner city—but we were still excited to be close to the biggest revolution in youth culture since rock and roll, a revolution that unites death and wealth in a troubled marriage.

1.8 MILLION BLACK MEN ARE MISSING

Nobody should be surprised that a popular subculture rooted in the lives of African-American men focuses so tightly on violence and death. About a third of African-American households enjoy annual incomes of $50,000 a year or more, but for the roughly one-quarter of African Americans who live in poverty, violence and death are a big part of everyday life.

One indicator of the disproportionate amount of violence faced by African-American men is the **sex ratio,** the number of men per 100 women in a population. In most of the world, the sex ratio is about 96. There are about 96 white American men for every 100 white American women, for example. More men than women work in dangerous jobs and engage in high-risk behavior such as smoking and excessive alcohol consumption. Besides, women are the hardier sex, biologically speaking. That's why there are fewer men than women in most populations.[1]

Among African Americans, however, the sex ratio is less than 87, an extraordinarily low figure. Assuming that a sex ratio of 96 is normal, we can conclude that 9 black men are missing for every 100 black women (because 96 minus 87 equals 9). Given 19.3 million black women in the United States in 2004, that works out to about 1.8 million missing black men. In 2004 there were 16.7 million black men in the United States but there should have been 18.5 million (calculated from U.S. Census Bureau, 2006).

Many missing black men died violently. The **homicide rate** is the number of murders per 100,000 people in a population. The black male homicide rate was nearly 39 in 2003 but reached about 60 in Illinois, Louisiana, and Pennsylvania. In contrast, the homicide rate was 5.7 for the United States as a whole and 1.7 for Canada. Figure 2.1 plots the homicide rate for black men against the black sex ratio for each state. It shows that in states where few black men are murdered, there are more black men than black women. But in states where many black men are murdered, there are many fewer black men than black women.[2]

---

1 Important exceptions exist. In much of Asia and North Africa, women suffer markedly poorer access to food and health services than men. In China, India, Singapore, Taiwan, and South Korea, ultrasound tests are widely used to determine the sex of babies before birth, and abortion of female fetuses is common. In such countries, the ratio of men to women is unusually high—about 106 (Brym and Lie, 2007: 588; Sen, 1990; 2001).

2 In Figure 2.1 and several other graphs in the book I include a "trend line" that summarizes the relationship between the two variables in the graph. Technically, the trend line is known as the **least-squares regression line.** It is a straight line in a two-dimensional graph that is drawn so as to minimize the sum of the squared perpendicular distances between each data point and the line itself.

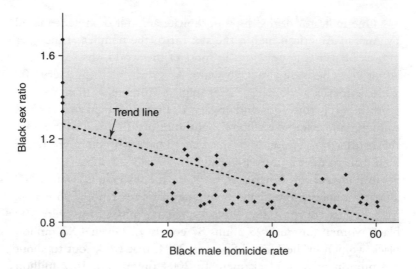

FIGURE 2.1   Male Homicide and the Sex Ratio by State, African Americans, 2003

Note: The black male homicide rate is the number of black men murdered per 100,000 black men in each state. The black male/female sex ratio is the number of black men divided by the number of black women in each state. Montana and Wyoming have been omitted because they are outliers and accounted for just 4 black homicides out of 7,083 in the United States in 2003.

SOURCE: Compiled from National Center for Injury Prevention and Control (2006); U.S. Census Bureau (2006).

In 2003, nearly 6,000 more black men than black women were murdered in the United States. But homicide is not the only cause of excess deaths among black men. In addition, about 4,000 more black men than black women died accidentally, mainly due to car accidents and drug overdoses. About 2,500 more black men than black women died of AIDS. About 1,000 more black men than black women committed suicide (calculated from National Center for Injury Prevention and Control, 2006; Kubrin, Wadsworth, and DiPitero, 2006). These figures oblige us to conclude that the destruction of the lives of poor African-American men by violence and high-risk behavior is horrifyingly routine. It is therefore to be expected that violence and death would form central themes in their cultural expression.

SOCIAL ORIGINS OF HIP HOP[3]

The situation of the African-American community as a whole has improved since the 1960s. The civil rights movement created new educational, housing, and job opportunities for African Americans and resulted in the creation of a substantial black middle class. The United States became a more tolerant and less discriminatory society. Yet in the midst of overall improvement, the situation of the roughly one-quarter of African Americans who live in poverty became bleaker.

After World War II, and especially in the 1960s, millions of southern blacks migrated to northern and western cities. Many were unable to find jobs. In some census tracts in Detroit, Chicago, Baltimore, and Los Angeles, black unemployment ranged from 26 to 41 percent in 1960. Many of the migrants were single women under the age of 25. Many had children but lacked a husband and a high school diploma.

The race riots of the 1960s helped to persuade the government to launch a "war on poverty" that increased the welfare rolls. In 1973, the American poverty rate fell to 11.1 percent, its lowest point ever. After 1973, however, everything went downhill. Manufacturing industries left the inner city for suburban or foreign locales where land values were lower and labor was less expensive. In the three decades following 1973, the proportion of the American labor force employed in industry fell from about one-third to one-fifth. Unemployment among African-American youth rose to more than 40 percent. Middle-class blacks left the inner city for the suburbs. This migration robbed the remaining young people of successful role models. It also eroded the taxing capacity of municipal governments, leading to a decline in public services. Meanwhile, the American public elected conservative governments at the state and federal levels. They cut school and welfare budgets, thus deepening the destitution of ghetto life (Piven and Cloward, 1977: 264–361, 1993; Wilson, 1987).

With few legitimate prospects for advancement, poor African Americans turned increasingly to crime and, in particular, the drug

---

3 This and the next two sections are revised versions of an article that first appeared online as "Hip Hop from Dissent to Commodity" at www.societyinquestion4e.nelson .com/article1.html.

trade. In the late 1970s, cocaine was expensive and demand for the drug was flat. So in the early 1980s, Colombia's Medellin drug cartel introduced a less-expensive form of cocaine called rock or crack. Crack was inexpensive, it offered a quick and intense high, and it was highly addictive. Crack cocaine offered many people a temporary escape from hopelessness and soon became wildly popular in the inner city. Turf wars spread as gangs tried to outgun each other for control of the local traffic. The sale and use of crack became so widespread it corroded much of what was left of the inner-city African-American community (Davis, 1990).

The shocking conditions described above gave rise to a shocking musical form: hip hop. Stridently at odds with the values and tastes of both whites and middle-class African Americans, hip hop described and glorified the mean streets of the inner city while holding the police, the mass media, and other pillars of society in utter contempt. Furthermore, hip hop tried to offend middle-class sensibilities, black and white, by using highly offensive language.

In 1988, more than a decade after its first stirrings, hip hop reached its political high point with the release of the CD *It Takes a Nation of Millions to Hold Us Back* by Chuck D and Public Enemy. In "Don't Believe the Hype," Chuck D (Carlton Douglas Ridenhour) accused the mass media of maliciously distributing lies. In "Black Steel in the Hour of Chaos," he charged the FBI and the CIA with assassinating the two great leaders of the African-American community in the 1960s, Martin Luther King and Malcolm X. In "Party for Your Right to Fight," he blamed the federal government for organizing the fall of the Black Panthers, the radical black nationalist party of the 1960s. Here, it seemed, was an angry expression of subcultural revolt that could not be mollified.

Hip Hop Transformed

There were elements in hip hop that soon transformed it, however (Bayles, 1994: 341–62; Neal, 1999: 144–48). For one thing, early, radical hip hop was not written as dance music. It therefore cut itself off from a large audience. Moreover, hip hop entered a self-destructive phase with the emergence of gangsta rap, which extolled criminal lifestyles, denigrated women, and replaced politics with drugs, guns, and machismo. The release of Ice T's "Cop Killer" in 1992 provoked strong political opposition from Republicans and Democrats, white church groups, and black middle-class associations. "Cop Killer" was not hip hop, but it fueled a reaction against all antiestablishment music. Time/Warner was forced to withdraw the song from circulation. The sense that hip hop had reached a dead end, or at least a turning point, grew in 1996, when rapper Tupac Shakur was murdered in the culmination of a feud between two hip hop record labels, Death Row in Los Angeles and Bad Boy in New York (Springhall, 1998: 149–51).

If these events made it seem that hip hop was self-destructing, the police and insurance industries helped to speed up its demise. In 1988, a group called Niggaz with Attitude released "Fuck tha Police," a critique of police violence against black youth. Law enforcement officials in several cities dared the group to perform the song in public, threatening to detain the performers or shut down their shows. Increasingly thereafter, ticket holders at hip hop concerts were searched for drugs and weapons, and security was tightened. Insurance companies, afraid of violence, substantially raised insurance rates for hip hop concerts, making them a financial risk. Soon, the number of venues willing to sponsor hip hop concerts dwindled.

While the developments noted above did much to mute the political force of hip hop, the seduction of big money did more. As early as 1982, with the release of Grandmaster Flash and the Furious Five's "The Message," hip hop began to win acclaim from mainstream rock music critics. With the success of Run-DMC and Public Enemy in the late 1980s, it became clear there was a big audience for hip hop. Significantly, much of that audience was composed of white youths. As one music critic wrote, they "relished ... the subversive 'otherness' that the music and its purveyors represented" (Neal, 1999: 144). Sensing the opportunity for profit, major media corporations, such as Time/Warner, Sony, CBS/Columbia, and BMG Entertainment, signed distribution deals with the small independent recording labels that had formerly been the exclusive distributors of hip hop CDs. In 1988, *Yo! MTV Raps* debuted. The program brought hip hop to middle America.

Most hip hop recording artists proved they were eager to forego political relevancy for commerce. For instance, Wu–Tang Clan started a line of clothing called Wu Wear, and, with the help of major hip hop recording artists, companies as diverse as Tommy Hilfiger, Timberland, Starter, and Versace began to market clothing influenced by ghetto styles. Independent labels, such as Phat Farm and Fubu, also prospered. The members of Run–DMC once said that they "don't want nobody's name on my behind" but those days were long past. By the early 1990s, hip hop was no longer just a musical form but a commodity with spin-offs. Rebellion had been turned into mass consumption.

Diddy

No rapper did a better job of turning rebellion into a commodity than Sean John Combs, better known as Puff Daddy, later as P. Diddy, and, as of 2005, Diddy. Diddy was born into a middle-class family in a New York suburb, became an avid Boy Scout, attended private school, played high school football, and then enrolled in Washington DC's Howard University, the leading black university in the United States. Yet, despite his background, he seems to promote rebellion. For example, the liner notes for his 1999 CD, *Forever,* proclaim a revolution led by rebels, rule-breakers, and mavericks. Diddy says that by asserting your unique brand of individuality, you can change the world.

Note, however, that he encourages only individual acts of rebellion, not radical, collective, political solutions. His politics became so mainstream that he was a prominent activist in the "get out the vote" campaign for the 2004 presidential election. Diddy's brand of dissent thus appeals to a broad audience, much of it white and middle-class. As his video director, Martin Weitz, observed in an interview for *Elle* magazine, Diddy's market is not the inner city: "No ghetto kid from Harlem is going to buy Puffy. They think he sold out. It's more like the 16-year-old white girls in the Hamptons, baby!" (quoted in Everett-Green, 1999).

It is also important to note that Diddy encourages individual acts of rebellion only to the degree that they enrich him and the media conglomerate he works for.[4] And rich he has become. Diddy lives in a multimillion-dollar mansion on Park Avenue in Manhattan and a multimillion-dollar house in the Hamptons. In 2005, *Forbes* magazine ranked him the twentieth most important celebrity in the United States and the third biggest money earner among musicians, with an annual income of $36 million ("The Celebrity 100," 2005). Diddy is entirely forthright about his self-enriching aims. In his 1997 song, "I Got the Power," Diddy referred to himself as "that nigga with the gettin' money gameplan" (Combs and the Lox, 1997). And in *Forever*, he reminds us: "Nigga get money, that's simply the plan." From this point of view, Diddy has more in common with Martha Stewart than with Chuck D and Public Enemy (Everett-Green, 1999).

BLING

Some hip hop artists come from the inner city, have criminal backgrounds, served time in prison, and glorify the gangster lifestyle. As of this writing, Curtis "50 Cent" Jackson is probably the best known among them. Some hip hop artists remain true to their political birthright. For example, Chuck D's mother was a Black Panther activist, and to this day he is engaged in raising black political consciousness as a writer, publisher, and producer. It seems, however, that a large number of prominent hip hop artists emulate the gangster lifestyle neither because it reflects their origins nor because they regard it as a political statement but simply because it is stylish and profitable to do so. Their backgrounds have nothing in common with drug suppliers, pimps, and gang leaders, and their politics are mainstream or nonexistent.

Even in the early years of hip hop, a gap between the biographies of many hip hop artists and their public personae was evident for those who took the time to do a background check. Three examples:

- DMC (Darryl McDaniels) was part of the legendary Run-DMC, the first hip hop group that looked like it ran with a gang and had

---

4 *Forever* is marketed, manufactured, and distributed by a unit of BMG Entertainment, the multibillion-dollar entertainment division of Germany's Bertelsmann AG, the third-largest media company in the world.

just come off the street corner. Run-DMC was credited with bringing hip hop into the mainstream in the 1980s. Yet DMC was born into a solidly middle-class, suburban family. His parents were college-educated. He was described by rock critic Bill Adler as a good Catholic school kid, a mama's boy (Samuels, 2004: 149).

- Another infamous figure was Ice T (Tracy Marrow). He is often credited with starting the gangsta rap movement with his single, "6'n the Morning." He released "Cop Killer" in 1992, causing a national scandal. Yet Ice T completed high school and served in the Army as a ranger in the 25th Infantry. He now continues serving the forces of good by playing a detective in the TV show *Law and Order: Special Victims Unit*.

- Flavor Flav (William Jonathan Drayton, Jr.) was a member of the notorious Chuck D band Public Enemy. Yet he graduated high school and attended Adelphi, an old, respected college in Long Island, New York. He trained as a classical pianist. After a stint on the reality TV show, *The Surreal Life 3*, he made a living co-starring in another reality TV show, *Strange Love,* with Brigitte Nielsen, a Danish actress once married to Sylvester Stallone. His next TV venture was *The Flavor of Love,* in which 20 single women who professed to adore him moved into a "phat crib" in Los Angeles and competed for his affections.

My contention that the "gettin' money gameplan" drives many hip hop artists is supported by the near-worship of luxury commodities in much of their music. Consider Tables 2.1 and 2.2, based on the top 20 song of 2005 on the Billboard charts, almost all of which were in the hip hop genre. Table 2.1 shows how many times the ten most frequently mentioned brands were referred to in the top 20 songs. Table 2.2 lists the eight recording artists who referred to brands most frequently. The numbers tell a fascinating story. Each of the top 20 songs of 2005 mentioned brands 25.5 times on average. Assuming the average song is 3 minutes long, that works out to a brand mentioned every 7 seconds. From this point of view, hip hop is a lot like one of those soap commercials that rely mainly on brand-name repetition to ensure that consumers keep the product in mind when they go grocery shopping.

TABLE 2.1 Brand Names in Top 20 Songs, 2005

Brand	Number of Mentions
Mercedes-Benz automobile	100
Nike sports shoes	63
Cadillac automobile	62
Bentley automobile	51
Rolls-Royce automobile	46
Hennessy cognac	44
Chevrolet automobile	40
Louis Vuitton luggage	35
Cristal champagne	35
AK-47 assault rifle	33
Total	509
Average mentions/song	25.5

SOURCE: Adapted from Agenda Inc. (2006): 4–7.

TABLE 2.2 Top Brand Name-Dropping Artists, 2005

Artist	Number of Mentions
50 Cent	20 brands in 7 songs
Ludacris	13 brands in 6 songs
The Game	13 brands in 2 songs
Ciara	10 brands in 4 songs
Jamie Foxx	6 brands in 1 song
Kanye West	6 brands in 1 song
Lil' Jon	6 brands in 2 songs
Trick Daddy	6 brands in 2 songs
Total	80 brands in 25 songs
Average brands/song	3.2

SOURCE: Adapted from Agenda Inc. (2006): 4–7.

In the world of hip hop, however, the good life is strongly associated not with laundry detergent but with driving a Mercedes, wearing Nikes, drinking Hennessy cognac, and packing an AK-47.

STREET CRED

The runaway financial success of some hip hop artists can rob them of what they call "street cred." One's claim to be a pimp or a cop killer can lose credibility when one shops at Salvatore Ferragamo and lives in the suburbs.

Successful hip hop artists have responded to the problem of street cred in three ways. First, some decide to give up any pretense of street cred by using their money to insulate themselves from the inner city. A Diddy or a Will Smith (formerly the Fresh Prince) makes no bones about catering to a largely white, suburban, culturally and politically mainstream, middle-class audience. They never lived in the inner city and apparently have no plans to visit anytime soon.

Successful hip hop artists whose audience appeal derives from their self-characterization as street toughs often take a more dangerous tack. They may live in the wealthy suburbs but continue to frequent the inner city, where some of them were born. Many of them are undoubtedly nostalgic about inner-city life, but they seem also to be motivated to visit the clubs and street corners of their old 'hood to show that they have not sold out. The trouble is that permanent residents often envy their wealth and fame, and this resentment can easily boil over into lethal violence. Famous hip hop artists who were shot and killed visiting their old neighborhoods after striking it rich include Scott La Rock (Scott Sterling) in 1987 (the first high-profile hip hop slaying), Run-DMC's Jam Master Jay (Jason Mizell) in 2002, and Proof (DeShaun Holton), Eminem's right-hand man and member of D-12 in 2006 (Dawsey, 2006).

A compromise between rejecting the inner city and visiting it as a rich tourist involves staging gun battles for public consumption. For example, in March 2005, a sidewalk gun fight broke out near hip hop radio station WQHT in New York City between the entourages of hip hop star The Game and his former mentor, 50 Cent. The Game had hinted that he might record with one of 50 Cent's rivals, so 50

Cent expelled The Game from his inner circle. The gunfight followed. Four years earlier, on the same street corner, a similar incident occurred between followers of Lil' Kim, one of the few female hip hop stars, and rival Capone after Capone's group had referred to Lil' Kim as "lame" in their appropriately titled song, "Bang, Bang." In both gunfights, the hip hop stars' followers discharged many rounds of ammunition at close range but damage was minor. Total casualties in the 2001 and 2005 gun battles combined: one man shot in the leg in 2005.

It seems plausible that the gunfights were actually for show. They helped to reinforce the violent image and street cred of the hip hop stars involved. Hip hop stars are multimillionaire members of the music elite, but the gunfights confer "the illusion of their authenticity as desperate outlaws" (Hajdu, 2005). In that light, shootouts are low-risk investments by savvy businesspeople. Lil' Kim's shootout certainly paid off handsomely. She claimed in front of a Grand Jury that two of her associates were not present at the 2001 gunfight. But witnesses contradicted her testimony and WQHT's security tape showed her holding a door open for one of the men. She was subsequently sentenced to a year and a day in prison for perjury. The two weeks preceding her imprisonment were videotaped for a reality show on Black Entertainment Television. The first episode of *Lil' Kim: Countdown to Lockdown* was the most watched series debut in the network's 25-year history. It has not been disclosed how much Lil' Kim earned for her efforts (Associated Press, 2005; Strong, 2006).

THE THREE PROMISES OF HIP HOP

Identity

[M]an ain't like a dog . . . because . . . he know about death. . . . [W]e ain't gonna get no move on in this world, lyin' around in the sun, lickin' our ass all day . . . , [s]o with this said, you tell me what it is you wanna do with your life.

—DJAY (TERRENCE HOWARD), A PIMP, TO NOLA (TARYN
MANNING), ONE OF HIS PROSTITUTES, IN *HUSTLE
AND FLOW* (2005)

People create, share, and socially transmit languages, beliefs, symbols, values, material objects, routine practices, and art forms to help them survive and prosper. Sociologists call the sum total of these responses to real-life problems **culture**. Medicine, Christianity, the Russian language, and the pulley help people cope, respectively, with ill health, questions about the meaning of life, the desire to communicate, and the need to raise heavy objects. Hip hop is no different. It is also a response to real-life problems (Swidler, 1986).

For example, the 2005 box-office hit, *Hustle and Flow,* tells the story of how DJay responds culturally to his life problems. Knowing that we will die, we must choose how to live meaningfully or be reduced to an existence little better than that of a dog, says DJay. He finds that he can achieve self-fulfillment by giving up his life as a pimp and giving voice to the joys and frustrations of the life he knows in the largely black, poor, violent, downtown core of Memphis, Tennessee. He becomes a hip hop artist. Artistic self-expression renders his life meaningful and rewarding. It gives him a sense of identity.

To operate in the world, people must develop a sense of who they are and what they can do (and who they aren't and what they can't do). The construction of identity is a lifelong task; people may alter their occupational, religious, national, ethnic, and even sexual identity as they mature and their circumstances change. But adolescence is the stage of life when most people lay the foundation for future development. It is typically a turbulent period, full of tentative experiments, exuberant strivings, emulation of heroes, self-doubt, false starts, and confrontation with stubborn authority. By means of these experiments, strivings, and so forth, adolescents form a baseline identity. Particular styles of popular music—unique patterns of rhythm, melody, and lyrics—express adolescent struggles in particular social contexts and give them form. That is why popular music is so meaningful and important to most adolescents (and nostalgic adults) (Gracyk, 2001).

Minor currents in hip hop oppose violence, crime, drugs, and the mistreatment of women, but the dominant identity promoted by the genre is that of proud, arrogant, violent, criminal, misogynistic, black hypermasculinity. The identity is largely a response to the degrading effects of perceived racism on the self-esteem of black men in the

American inner city. Take persistent poverty and bad schools, remove social services and industrial jobs, introduce crack and gang wars, and you soon get hip hop (Dyson, 2005). Nelson George, the genre's leading historian, writes that hip hop is "a system of survival" and "an invigorating source of self-empowerment" (George, 1999: 50). It negates middle-class sensibilities because many black men believe that middle-class sensibilities have tried to negate them.

Upward Mobility

George is correct to note that "hip hop didn't start as a career move but as a way of announcing one's existence in the world" (George, 1999: 14). Nonetheless, a career move it soon became. If hip hop's first promise was to provide a sense of black male identity in the context of the American inner city in the 1970s and 1980s, its second promise was to serve as a path of upward social mobility out of that context. (**Upward mobility** refers to advancement within a system of inequality.)

Yet hip hop's lure resembles the largely false hope offered by professional sports. In 2004, the National Basketball Association, the National Football League, and Major League Baseball employed 3,911 players, of whom 1,650 were black (see Table 2.3). That's 1,650 out of roughly 5 million black men between the ages of 18 and 40. The odds of an African-American man in the 18–40 age cohort being a top professional athlete are 3,030 to 1. If he lives to the age of 80, he has a better chance (3,000 to 1) of getting struck by lightning in his lifetime (estimated from "Facts about Lightning," 2006; U.S. Census Bureau, 2002b). Although I have not been able to find statistics on the subject, it is evident that the odds of an African-American man becoming a hip hop star are considerably worse than his odds of becoming a top professional athlete; the black men who become well-known hip hop artists even at the regional level, let alone nationally or internationally, number in the low hundreds, not the low thousands.

The poor black youth who regard professional athletes and hip hop artists as role and mobility models have little chance of realizing their dreams, all the more so because their unrealistic aspirations often deflect their attention from a much safer bet: staying in school,

TABLE 2.3 African-American Men in Professional Sports, 2004

Sport	Players	Black players	Blacks as percent of total
National Football League	1,842	1,228	67
National Basket-ball Association	478	311	65
Major League Baseball	1,591	111	7
Total	3,911	1,650	42

NOTE: The disproportionately large number of black players in the NBA and the NFL is sometimes used to defend the view that blacks are *genetically* superior athletes (Entine, 2000). However, no genetic evidence of black athletic superiority exists. Besides, non-blacks dominate many sports, including hockey (Canadians and Russians), swimming (Australians), gymnastics (East Europeans and Chinese), and soccer (West Europeans and South Americans). Superiority of particular racial, ethnic, and national groups in certain sports is the result of unique combinations of climate, geography, history, culture, and government and private-sector sponsorship, not genes.

SOURCE: Richard Lapchick. 2004. 2004 Racial and Gender Report Card. Orlando, FL: University of Central Florida. Pp. 15, 26, 35. Found at: www.bus.ucf.edu/sport/public/downloads/2004_Racial_Gender_Report_Card.pdf. (Accessed 29 April, 2006)

studying hard, and pursuing an ordinary career (Doberman, 1997). The odds of an African-American man in the 18–40 age cohort being a physician are roughly seven times better than the odds of his being a professional athlete or a well-known hip hop artist, and the odds of his being a lawyer are roughly 14 times better (estimated from Holmes, 2005; King and Bendel, 1995; U.S. Census Bureau, 2002a). Yet because so many young African-American men seek to follow the career paths and emulate the lifestyles (including the criminality) of a 50 Cent or an Allen Iverson, too few of them sing the praises of Dr. James McCune Smith, the first African-American doctor, or seek to emulate the uncool but respectable accomplishments of TV's Dr. Heathcliff Huxtable (Bill Cosby's character in *The Cosby Show,* which ran from 1984 to 1992). In 2005, the number of black law students in the United States fell to a 12-year low despite a growing black population (Holmes, 2005).

An important lesson about the nature of culture lies embedded in this story. Culture is created to solve human problems, as we have seen. But not all elements of culture solve problems equally well. Some elements of culture even create new problems. After all, the creators of culture are only human. In the case at hand, it seems that by promoting unrealistic hopes for upward mobility and encouraging a lifestyle that draws young African-American men away from school, hard work, and the pursuit of an ordinary career, hip hop culture badly shortchanges them.

Power

Like hip hop's promise of upward mobility, its assurance of power has proven largely an illusion.

We saw that hip hop emerged among African-American inner-city youth as a cry of despair with strong political overtones. Many commentators believed that by reflecting the traditions, frustrations, and ambitions of the community that created it, hip hop would help the otherwise isolated voices of poor black youth sing in unison, shape a collective identity, and engage in concerted political action to improve the conditions of all African Americans (Mattern, 1998).

There are still radical political currents in hip hop. For the most part, however, it has become an apolitical commodity that increasingly appeals to a heterogeneous but mainly white, middle-class audience. As one of hip hop's leading analysts and academic sympathizers writes, "The discourse of ghetto reality or 'hood authenticity remains largely devoid of political insight or progressive intent" (Forman, 2001: 121).

Hip hop substantially lost its politics for three reasons. First, as one industry insider notes, "Mainstream media outlets and executive decision-makers . . . fail to encourage or support overt political content and militant ideologies because . . . 'it upsets the public' " (KRS-One cited in Forman, 2001: 122). The recording industry got excited about hip hop precisely when executives saw the possibility of "crossover," that is, selling the new black genre in the much larger white community. For them, hip hop was an opportunity little different from that offered by Motown in the 1960s. They apparently understood well, however, that to turn hip hop into an appealing mass-marketed commodity it had to be tamed and de-clawed of its political content so as not to offend its large potential audience. If recording industry executives and hip hop artists needed further motivation to tone down the rhetoric, the political opposition to hip hop that was stimulated by gangsta rap and songs like "Cop Killer" in the early 1990s certainly helped. That opposition was the second reason hip hop lost its politics. Third, hip hop artists themselves contributed to the de-politicization of their music. For the most part untutored in politics, history, and sociology, they are not equipped to think clearly and deeply about public policies that could help the black underclass and the specific forms of political action that could get the black underclass to help itself. At most, they offer the flavor of rebelliousness, the illusion of dissent, giving members of their audience the feeling of being daring and notorious rule breakers and revolutionaries but offering nothing in the way of concrete ideas, let alone leadership.

Vladimir Lenin, leader of the Russian Revolution of 1917, once said that capitalists are so eager to earn profits that they will sell the rope from which they themselves will hang. But he underestimated his opponents. Savvy executives and willing recording artists have taken the edge off hip hop to make it more appealing to a mass market, thus turning dissent into a commodity (Frank and Weiland, 1997). Young consumers are fooled into thinking they are buying rope to hang owners of big business, political authorities, and cultural conservatives. In reality, they're just buying rope to constrain themselves.

CULTURE AND SOCIAL STRUCTURE

Social structures are relatively stable patterns of social relations that create opportunities for and constrain thought and action. For example, in a social structure composed of just two people, both individuals must be engaged for the structure to persist. If one person fails to participate and contribute to the satisfaction of the other, the relationship will soon dissolve. In contrast, three-person social structures are generally more stable because one person may mediate conflict between the other two. In addition, three-person structures allow one person to exploit rivalry between the other two in order to achieve dominance. Thus, the introduction of a third person makes possible a new set of social dynamics that are impossible in a two-person structure (Simmel, 1950). What is true for two- and three-person relationships holds for social structures composed of millions of people that are organized into institutions, racial groups, social classes, and entire societies; they constrain and create a host of opportunities for the people who constitute them.

Sociologists have long debated whether social structure gives rise to culture or vice versa. At first glance, this may seem to be a chicken-and-egg problem. For instance, in this chapter I have argued that the social structure of the American inner city gave rise to the cultural phenomenon of hip hop. But I have also argued that the culture of hip hop, insofar as it diverts attention from realistic avenues of social mobility and encourages violence, causes the social structure of the American inner city to persist. Chicken or egg?

Research on Media Violence

Since the 1960s, social scientists have employed the full range of sociological methods to investigate the effects of the mass media on real-world behavior. Most of their research focuses on *violent* behavior, and it's worth reviewing because it can improve our understanding of the relationship between hip hop culture and inner-city social structure.

Some of the research is based on **experiments**—carefully controlled artificial situations that allow researchers to isolate presumed causes and measure their effects precisely. In a typical experiment, a group of children is randomly divided into "experimental" and "control" groups. The experimental group is shown a violent TV program. The level of aggressiveness of both groups at play is measured before and after the showing. If, after the showing, members of the experimental group play significantly more aggressively than they did before the showing, and significantly more aggressively than members of the control group, the researchers conclude that TV violence affects real-world behavior.

Scores of such experiments show that exposure to media violence increases violent behavior in young children, especially boys, over the short term. Results are mixed when it comes to assessing longer term effects, especially on older children and teenagers (Anderson and Bushman, 2002; Browne and Hamilton-Giachritsis, 2005; Freedman, 2002).

Sociologists have also used **surveys** to measure the effects of media violence on behavior. In a survey, randomly selected people are asked questions about their knowledge, attitudes, or behavior.

Researchers aim to study part of a group (a **sample**) to learn about the whole group of interest (the **population**). The results of most surveys show a significant relationship between exposure to violent mass media and violent behavior, albeit a weaker relationship than experiments show. Some surveys, however, find no relationship (Anderson and Bushman, 2002; Huesmann, Moise-Titus, Podolski, and Eron, 2003; Johnson, Cohen, Smailes, Kasen, and Brook, 2002).

Field research—systematically observing people in their natural social settings—has also been employed to help us understand how media violence may influence behavior. For example, sociologists have spent time in schools where shooting rampages have taken place. They have developed a deep appreciation of the context of school shootings by living in the neighborhoods where they occur, interviewing students, teachers, neighborhood residents, and shooters' family members, and studying police and psychological reports, the shooters' own writings, and other relevant materials (Harding, Fox, and Mehta, 2002; Sullivan, 2002). They have tentatively concluded that only a small number of young people—those who are weakly connected to family, school, community, and peers—are susceptible to translating media violence into violent behavior. Lack of social support allows their personal problems to become greatly magnified, and if guns are readily available, they are prone to using violent media messages as models for their own behavior. In contrast, for the overwhelming majority of young people, violence in the mass media is just a source of entertainment and a fantasy outlet for emotional issues, not a template for action (Anderson, 2003).

Finally, **official statistics** (numerical data originally compiled by state organizations for purposes other than sociological research) have been analyzed to place the effects of media violence on real-world behavior into broader perspective. For example, researchers have discovered big differences in violent behavior between the United States and Canada. The homicide rate (the number of murders per 100,000 people) has historically been about three to four times higher in the United States. Yet TV programming, movies, and video games are nearly identical in the two countries, so exposure to media violence can't account for the difference. Most researchers attribute the difference to the higher level of economic and social inequality and the wider availability of handguns in the United States (Government of Canada, 2002; Lenton, 1989; National Rifle Association, 2005).

My literature review leads me to unscramble this particular chicken-and-egg debate as follows. Media violence in general, and hip hop culture in particular, probably stimulates real-world violence among a minority of young people, although to a considerably lesser degree than some alarmists would have us believe (McWhorter, 2005: 315–51). The effects are strongest among male adolescents who lack strong ties to family and other institutions that, by example, instruction, and discipline, typically socialize young people to refrain from violence. The effects are especially exaggerated in settings where economic and social inequality is high and where handguns are readily available.

The effects of the mass media on *nonviolent* behavior are probably more widespread and stronger. After all, parents, teachers, and religious figures spend a lot of time and effort teaching children and adolescents that violence is in most cases morally wrong. Along with the police and the courts, they impose severe penalties on youth who act violently. In contrast, while parents and teachers may look askance at a pair of pants that hang far below the waist, few people are likely to impose penalties for wearing them. That's why the mass media probably exert more influence over lifestyle than violence.

I conclude that hip hop culture probably does a more effective job of getting young people to dress and talk in certain ways and misguiding them about their mobility prospects than it does of influencing them to act violently. It follows that social reformers interested in lowering levels of violence can achieve little by bashing hip hop culture. They could lower the level of violence a lot more effectively by figuring out ways to limit the availability of handguns and shore up or provide alternatives to faltering social institutions in the inner city, especially schools and families.

CRITICAL THINKING EXERCISES

1. What do you personally gain from hip hop? How are you negatively affected by hip hop? Do the positive influences outweigh the negative influences or vice versa? After drawing up a

balance sheet for yourself, create a similar balance sheet for your society as a whole. How, if at all, does your personal balance sheet differ from your societal balance sheet?

2. In one page, explain why, in your opinion, different research methods reach somewhat different conclusions about the effects of media violence on real-world behavior. How can the research method itself influence the results of the research?

3. Some analysts argue that social conditions are wholly responsible for the behavior of people. Others argue that people are responsible for their own behavior. Still others hold that while social conditions influence behavior, people still have plenty of room for choice and therefore bear some responsibility for their actions. In two pages, justify your position. Make your case based on the example of African Americans.

3

✳

Explaining Suicide Bombers[1]

FROM KARBALA TO MEKHOLA

"Ya Karbala! Ya Hussein! Ya Khomeini!" That was the cry of waves of Iranian children and youths armed with Kalashnikovs and hand grenades as they attacked Iraqi positions during the early years of the Iran-Iraq war (1980–1988). Entrenched machine guns and helicopter gunships mowed them down, but new waves kept coming. They fought for Karbala, the town where, in 680 CE,[2] a battle took place between factions that disagreed over how they should choose the successor to the prophet Muhammad. The Sunni wanted the successor to be elected from a certain tribe, while the Shi'ites wanted him to be Muhammad's direct descendant. The youthful suicide attackers in the Iran-Iraq war also fought in the name of Hussein, the prophet Muhammad's grandson, who led the vastly outnumbered Shi'ites in their suicidal battle against the attacking Sunni at Karbala. Finally, they fought for Khomeini, the spiritual and political leader of Shi'ite Iran in the early 1980s. Lacking weapons and a well-organized army,

1 Parts of this chapter are based on Brym (2007, 2008) and Brym and Araj (2006, 2008).
2 "CE" stands for "common era" and is now preferred over the ethnocentric "AD," which stands for *anno Domini* (Latin for "the year of our Lord").

Khomeini proclaimed it an honor to die in holy battle and instructed recruiters to find human cannon fodder in Iran's schools. In this way, suicide attacks were institutionalized as a technique of collective violence in the modern Islamic world.

Suicide attacks were molded into a precision instrument shortly afterward, when 2,000 Iranian Revolutionary Guard militants arrived in southern Lebanon to support the anti-Western and anti-Israel Hizballah movement (see Figure 3.1). The first suicide bombing against Western interests in the Middle East took place in Beirut, Lebanon, in October 1983, when Shi'ite militants attacked the military barracks of American and French peacekeepers, killing nearly 300 people. Four months later, Western troops fled the country, teaching the attackers that suicide bombings could not only be inexpensively organized, accurately directed, and precisely controlled, but that under some circumstances they could yield quick and substantial payoffs.

Israel invaded Lebanon in the summer of 1982 in an attempt to crush the Palestine Liberation Organization (PLO), which sought to recapture territory won by Israel in earlier wars (Brym, 1983; see Figure 3.2). The Israelis succeeded in forcing the PLO leadership out of Lebanon. However, the Iranian-backed Hizballah and several copycat groups used the presence of Israeli troops in Lebanon as an opportunity to launch more suicide attacks.

In 1985, Israel partially withdrew from Lebanon. It now sought to weaken the PLO in the West Bank and the Gaza Strip, territories it had occupied since its 1967 war with its Arab neighbors (see Figure 3.2). To that end, Israel permitted the establishment of a conservative Islamic organization—the Islamic Resistance Movement, or Hamas. It judged that the new organization would serve as a moderate political counterweight to the PLO. Israel let Hamas accept funding from Saudi Arabia, turned a blind eye as its supporters stormed cinemas and set fire to restaurants selling alcohol, and allowed the creation of the Islamic University of Gaza. Ironically, the university later became a recruiting ground for suicide bombers (Reuter, 2004: 98).

Hamas, in fact, became the leading proponent of suicide bombings inside Israel and its occupied territories. In April 1993, the first such attack took place in the rural Israeli settlement of Mekhola. Nineteen similar attacks were staged over the next four years in Israel,

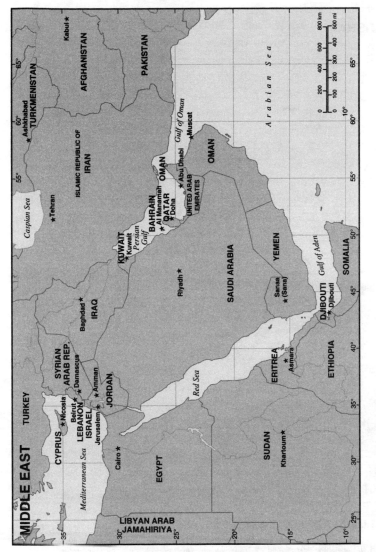

FIGURE 3.1 The Middle East

SOURCE: United Nations Cartographic Section. The Middle East. Map No. 4102. Rev. 3. United Nations. July 1997. Found at: http://www.un.org/Depts/Cartographic/map/profile/mideastr.pdf

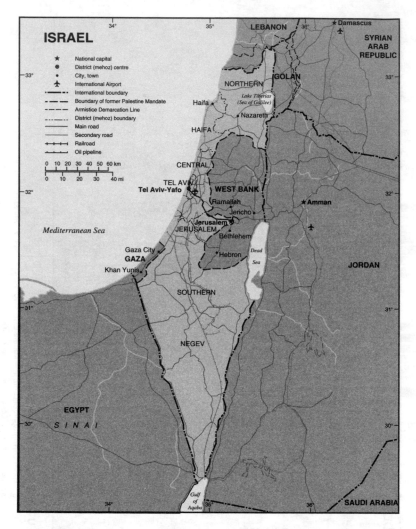

FIGURE 3.2   Israel, the West Bank, and Gaza

SOURCE: United Nations Cartographic Section. Southeastern Mediterranean. Map No. 4013.
United Nations. July 1997. Found at: http://www.un.org/Depts/Cartographic/map/profile/
semedite.pdf

the West Bank, and Gaza. Between 1993 and 1997, suicide bombers
were responsible for killing 175 people (including 21 suicide bombers)
and injuring 928 others (Johnston, 2003). A second and more lethal
wave of suicide bombings began on October 26, 2000. By April 18,

2006, suicide bombers were responsible for killing an additional 685 people (including 153 suicide bombers) and injuring 3,849 others (*al-Quds,* 2000–2005; *al-Quds al-'Arabi,* 2000–2005; International Policy Institute for Counter-Terrorism, 2004; Israeli Ministry of Foreign Affairs, 2004; *New York Times,* 2000–2006). In the early years of the twenty-first century, Israel, the West Bank, and Gaza became the region of the world with the highest frequency of, and the highest per capita death toll due to, suicide bombing.

EXPLANATIONS

Explanations for the rise of suicide bombing since the early 1980s focus on three sets of factors:

1. the characteristics of the suicide bombers;

2. the occupation, by perceived foreigners, of territory claimed by the suicide bombers and their organizations as their homeland; and

3. the interaction between perpetrators of suicide attacks and occupiers.

Let us examine each of these explanations in turn.

Focus on the Perpetrators

Psychopathology   Lance Corporal Eddie DiFranco is the only survivor of the 1983 suicide attack on the U.S. Marine barracks in Beirut who saw the face of the bomber. DiFranco was on watch when he noticed the attacker speeding his truck full of explosives toward the main building on the marine base. "He looked right at me [and] smiled," DiFranco recalls (quoted in Reuter, 2004: 53).

Many Western observers quickly passed a verdict: People willing to blow themselves up to kill others must be abnormal, and if they die happily they must surely be deranged. Thus, some psychologists characterized the Beirut bombers as "unstable individuals with a death wish," although they lacked any evidence of the bombers' state of mind (Perina, 2002). Similarly, following the September 11, 2001, suicide attacks on the United States, U.S. government and media interpretations underscored the supposed irrationality and even outright insanity of the bombers, again without the benefit of supporting data (Atran, 2003: 1535–36).

Despite such claims, interviews with prospective suicide bombers and reconstructions of the biographies of successful suicide bombers do not suggest a higher rate of psychopathology than in the general population (Davis, 2003; Reuter, 2004; Stern, 2003; Victor, 2003). A study of all 462 suicide bombers who attacked targets worldwide between 1980 and 2003 found not a single case of depression, psychosis, past suicide attempts, or other such disorders among them and only one case of probable mental retardation (Pape, 2005: 210). Evidence collected by other experts suggests that "recruits who display signs of pathological behavior are automatically weeded out for reasons of organizational security" (Taarnby, 2003: 18). It seems reasonable to conclude that individualistic explanations based on psychopathology are of no value in helping us understand the rising incidence of suicide bombing in the world.

Deprivation   A second explanation of suicide bombing that focuses on the characteristics of perpetrators is the deprivation argument. In this view, suicide bombers act because they suffer extreme deprivation, either absolute or relative. **Absolute deprivation** refers to longstanding poverty and unemployment. **Relative deprivation** refers to the growth of an intolerable gap between what people expect out of life and what they get out of it (Gurr, 1970). Presumably, deprivation of one sort or the other frustrates some categories of people until they are driven to commit self-destructive acts of aggression against the perceived source of their suffering.

Evidence does not support the deprivation theory. One researcher collected education and income data on about 30 percent of Arab suicide bombers between 1980 and 2003. He reported that they were much better educated than the populations from which they were recruited. They were typically from the working and middle classes and were seldom unemployed or poor (Pape, 2005: 213–15). Another scholar discovered that suicide bombers from Egypt and Saudi Arabia had come mainly from middle- or upper-middle-class families (Laqueur, 2004: 16). The perpetrators of the September 11, 2001, attacks on the

United States were well-educated, middle-class men. Such evidence lends no credence to the notion that suicide bombers are especially deprived in any absolute sense.

Arguments about relative deprivation are purely speculative. To date, no researcher has measured the degree to which suicide bombers are relatively deprived and compared their level of relative deprivation with that of non-suicide bombers. The consensus in the literature today is that suicide bombers do not experience extraordinarily high levels of deprivation, either relative or absolute (Stern, 2003: 50–52; Taarnby, 2003: 10–12; Victor, 2003).

Culture Explanations for suicide bombing that focus on the individual characteristics of the attackers began to fray in the late 1980s, partly because the evidence collected by researchers did not support them. Consequently, many analysts shifted their focus to the *collective* characteristics of suicide bombers and, in particular, their culture.

Some social scientists attributed much of the collective violence in the world to a "clash of civilizations" between Islam and the West (Huntington, 1996; for a critique, see Hunter, 1998). From their point of view, Islamic culture inclines Muslims to fanatic hatred of the West, violence, and, in the extreme case, suicide attacks. For example, the martyrdom of Hussein at the battle of Karbala in 680 CE was a signal event in Islamic history that is often said to have reinforced the readiness of Muslims, especially Shi'ites, to sacrifice their lives for the collective good in the face of overwhelming odds (Reuter, 2004: 37–39).

While such cultural resources likely increase the chance that some groups will engage in suicide attacks, one must be careful not to exaggerate their significance. One difficulty with the clash of civilizations thesis is that public opinion polls show that Arabs in the Middle East hold strongly favorable attitudes toward American science and technology, freedom and democracy, education, movies and television, and largely favorable attitudes toward the American people. They hold strongly negative attitudes only toward American Middle East policy (Zogby, 2002). This is less evidence of a clash of civilizations than a deep political disagreement.

Nor is the notion that an affinity exists between Islam and suicide bombing supported by most students of Islam. Thus, according to one such expert, "much of the so-called Islamic behavior that the West terms terrorism is outside the norms that Islam holds for political violence" (Silverman, 2002: 91).

One must also bear in mind that secular Muslim groups in the Middle East and non-Muslim groups outside the Middle East have employed suicide bombing as a tactic. The first suicide attack in recorded history involved a Western attack on Persian forces; one of the two Spartans who survived the battle of Thermopylae in 480 BCE went on a suicide mission against the Persian invaders. About 600 years later, Jewish Zealots embarked on suicide missions against Roman occupiers. In modern times, Japanese *kamikaze* pilots and *kaiten* torpedo riders were applauded for willingly sacrificing their lives in attacks on American vessels during World War II. The Viet Cong engaged in suicide attacks to liberate their homeland in the 1960s. The Liberation Tigers of Tamil Eelam in Sri Lanka—a Marxist and atheistic organization—accounted for 60 percent of the world's suicide attacks between 1983 and 2000. Among the 83 percent of suicide attackers between 1980 and 2003 for whom data on ideological background is available, only a minority—43 percent—were discernibly religious. Even in Lebanon, Israel, the West Bank, and Gaza between 1981 and 2003, fewer than half of suicide missions were conducted by deeply religious individuals. In sum, the notion that Islam predisposes its adherents to martyrdom ignores the non-Muslim traditions and the secular traditions in the Muslim world that have sometimes initiated and glorified similar acts (Boyle, 2006; Pape, 2005: 210; Ricolfi, 2005; Sprinzak, 2000).

A final difficulty with cultural interpretations is that suicide attacks are by no means a constant in Islamic history. They appear in eleventh-century northern Persia, in the eighteenth century in parts of India, Indonesia, and the Philippines, and in the late twentieth century in various parts of the Muslim world. The episodic nature of suicide attacks suggests that certain social and political circumstances may be decisive in determining which cultural resources are drawn upon at a given time to formulate tactics for collective violence. For example, in the eighteenth century suicide attacks were chosen as a tactic because little else proved effective against the vastly superior military forces of European and American colonial powers (Dale, 1988). Similarly, militant Islamic groups in the late twentieth and early twenty-first centuries adopted suicide bombing only after other tactics had met with failure. Suicide bombing, it seems, is a weapon of last resort. All of this points to the difficulty of trying to explain political variables with cultural constants.

Focus on the Occupiers

Although cultural explanations of suicide bombing still have their supporters, a shift of focus occurred in the late 1990s when scholars began to analyze suicide attacks as strategically rational political actions (Sprinzak, 2000). With the publication of Robert Pape's study of all 462 suicide bombers who attacked targets worldwide between 1980 and 2003, this school of thought was given a strong empirical basis of support (Pape, 2005).

According to Pape, every group mounting a suicide campaign since the early 1980s has shared one objective: to coerce a foreign state to remove its military forces from territory that group members view as their homeland (Pape, 2005: 21). Pape makes his case by first quoting the leaders of organizations that have mounted suicide attacks. They stated plainly and forcefully that their chief aim was to liberate territory from what they regarded as foreign occupation or control (Pape, 2005: 29–33). To support his claim that suicide bombing is a fundamentally rational strategy, Pape then notes that suicide attacks are not randomly distributed but occur in clusters as part of a campaign by an organized group to achieve a political goal. He identifies 18 suicide bombing campaigns that have taken place since the early 1980s, five of them ongoing (Pape, 2005: 40). Finally, Pape argues that the strategic rationality of suicide bombing is evident in the correlation between the increasing use of suicide bombing campaigns and their relative success in achieving their goals. He finds that suicide bombing has a roughly 50 percent success rate and regards that as high, since, by comparison, international military and economic coercion achieves its goals less than a third of the time (Pape, 2005: 65). In short, Pape claims that strategic rationality is evident in the *timing, objectives,* and *results* of suicide bombing campaigns.

Pape's research has convinced analysts that many instances of suicide bombing are not devoid of strategic logic. I contend, however, that it oversimplifies matters considerably to think that suicide bombing campaigns are launched only to liberate territory, that they are typically timed to maximize their impact in that regard, and that they often meet with success.

In the remainder of this chapter I analyze one of the three most protracted and destructive series of suicide bombings in the past quarter of a century—those of the second Palestinian *intifada* ("shaking off," or uprising) in Israel, the West Bank, and Gaza between 2000 and 2005. My analysis leads me to three conclusions:

1. First, with respect to *objectives:* Suicide bombing is an action that typically involves mixed motives and mixed organizational rationales. Strategic thinking is only one element that may combine with others in the creation of a suicide bomber. It predominates less frequently than Pape leads us to believe.

2. Second, with respect to *timing:* Because the individual motivations and organizational rationales of suicide bombings are often mixed, suicide bombing campaigns are not always or even often timed to maximize the strategic advantages of insurgents. The timing of suicide bombings may be detached from strategic considerations because they take place for nonstrategic reasons such as revenge or retaliation or simply when opportunities for attack happen to emerge. As a result, their timing may not maximize the strategic gains of the attackers and on occasion may even minimize such gains.

3. Third, with respect to *results:* suicide bombing campaigns sometimes encourage targets to make minor concessions, but they often fail to achieve their main objectives. Sometimes they have consequences that are the opposite of those intended by suicide attackers and their organizations. If suicide bombing pays, as Pape claims, its net returns are often meager and sometimes negative.

Suicide Bombing during the Second *Intifada*

One of my PhD students and I collected information on all 138 suicide bombings that took place in Israel, the West Bank, and Gaza from October 26, 2000, to July 12, 2005 (Brym and Araj, 2006). Our sources included the online database of the International Policy Institute for Counter-Terrorism (ICT) in Israel; the website of Israel's Ministry of Foreign Affairs; the East Coast evening edition of *The New York Times*; and two authoritative Arabic newspapers—*al-Quds,* published in Jerusalem, and *al-Quds al-'Arabi,* published in London. I was especially interested in three issues: (1) The reasons suicide bombers gave for their actions in public statements they made prior to attacking (that is, the bombers' *motives*); (2) the reasons that representatives of organizations claiming responsibility for suicide attacks gave for their actions (that is, the organizations' *rationales*); and (3) the specific preceding events that affected the timing of suicide bombings according to representatives of organizations claiming responsibility for the attacks (that is, the attacks' *precipitants*).

I classified the three causal mechanisms—bomber motives, organizational rationales, and event precipitants—as either "proactive" or "reactive." *Reactive* causes are Israeli actions that elicited a Palestinian reaction in the form of a suicide attack. Such Israeli actions include the assassination of organizational leaders and members, the killing of Palestinians other than organizational leaders and members, and other actions not involving killing, such as the demolition of houses owned by the families of people involved in anti-Israel activities. *Proactive* causes are political, religious, or ideological events that elicited a suicide attack without provocation by specific Israeli actions. In such cases, organizations used symbolically significant anniversaries, elections, or peace negotiations as opportunities to further their goals by means of suicide attacks.

I found that the great majority of suicide attacks during the second *intifada* were reactive: that is, provoked by specific Israeli actions (see Table 3.1). This finding has enormous implications for our understanding of the objectives, timing, and results of suicide bombing campaigns. Let us consider each of these issues in turn.

TABLE 3.1 Suicide Bombing and the Second *Intifada:* Causal Mechanisms (in percent)

Cause	Type		
	Reactive	Proactive	Total
Bomber motive (with implications for objectives)	71	30	101*
Organizational rationale (with implications for results)	59	41	100
Event precipitant (with implications for timing)	82	18	100

*Does not equal 100 because of rounding.
SOURCE: Adapted from Brym and Araj (2006).

Objectives   Revenge and retaliation figured prominently in the bombers' stated reasons for planning suicide attacks. For the most part, they gave up their lives not as part of some grand rational strategy, but to avenge the killing of a close relative, as retribution for specific attacks against the Palestinian people, or as payback for perceived attacks against Islam. This finding supports the educated but impressionistic conclusion reached by Israeli political philosopher Avishai Margalit:

> Having talked to many Israelis and Palestinians who know something about the bombers, and having read and watched many of the bombers' statements, my distinct impression is that the main motive of many of the suicide bombers is revenge for acts committed by Israelis, a revenge that will be known and celebrated in the Islamic world (Margalit, 2003).

Timing   The great majority of suicide attacks were precipitated by specific Israeli actions. Their timing was in that sense not of the Palestinians' choosing, and therefore not rationally planned to maximize strategic gains. To be sure, Israel's response to suicide bombings influenced the ease with which subsequent attacks could be mounted. Especially after the extraordinarily frequent and lethal suicide missions of March 2002, Israel's stepped-up counterterrorist activities significantly decreased the number of suicide bombings and increased the time between precipitant and reactive attack. But I found little evidence to support Pape's contention that suicide attacks are timed to maximize the achievement of strategic or tactical goals. My analysis of precipitants leads me to conclude that most suicide bombings were revenge or retaliatory attacks and were advertised as such by insurgents.

Results   Pape's claim that suicide bombing achieves a relatively high rate of success in terms of achieving strategic goals is also questionable. Pape defines success as the withdrawal of occupying forces. The second *intifada* witnessed just one such withdrawal—Israel's August/ September 2005 pullout from Gaza. Can the pullout be construed as a consequence of Palestinian suicide attacks?

Two facts argue against such an interpretation. First, when I examined the geographical locations of suicide bombings and the geographical origins of the bombers themselves, I found that Gaza was the site of a disproportionately small number of suicide attacks and the recruiting ground for a disproportionately small number of suicide bombers. If suicide attacks were a decisive factor in producing territorial concessions, one would expect those concessions to have been made not in Gaza but in the West Bank, where the great majority of bombers were recruited and from which the great majority of suicide attacks were launched.

Second, to the degree that militant Palestinian organizations mount suicide attacks to coerce Israel to abandon territory, the results of such attacks seem to be the opposite of what was intended. Rather than pushing the Israeli public to become more open to the idea of territorial concessions, suicide bombings have had the opposite effect. Israeli polls thus show that suicide attacks helped hardliner Ariel Sharon win the February 2001 election and, in general, drove Israeli public opinion to the right throughout the second *intifada* (Arian, 2001, 2002; Elran, 2006).

Suicide bombings also encouraged Israel to reoccupy Palestinian population centers in the West Bank and Gaza. Israel had withdrawn from those population centers in 1995–1997 as a result of peace talks. But in March 2002, 135 Israeli civilians were killed in suicide attacks, the most infamous of which was the so-called Passover massacre at the Park Hotel in Netanya, in which 30 Israelis lost their lives. Within

24 hours, Israel launched Operation Defensive Shield. Twenty thousand reservists were called up in the biggest mobilization since the 1982 invasion of Lebanon and the biggest military operation in the West Bank and Gaza since the 1967 war. The West Bank and Gaza were almost completely reoccupied by April. Even if the strategic aim of the suicide bombings in March was purely to coerce Israel to withdraw from the occupied territories, the result of those attacks was just the opposite. On a broader canvas, substantial West Bank territory has been incorporated on the Israeli side of the wall that Israel is building to make it harder to launch suicide attacks. Therefore, in the long run, too, suicide bombings will have made it more difficult for the Palestinians to gain territorial concessions from Israel. Many Palestinians themselves recognize that suicide bombing is a problematic strategy that rarely achieves strategic territorial goals and often has unintended, negative consequences from the Palestinian point of view. Among them is Palestinian President Mahmoud Abbas, who typically declares each suicide bombing "a crime against our people" ("al-Ra'is...," 2005).

Focus on the Interaction

How can we explain the rise of suicide bombing since the early 1980s? There seems little advantage in focusing on the characteristics of suicide bombers themselves. On close inspection, neither their mental state nor their supposed deprivation nor their alleged cultural background adequately accounts for their actions.

Focusing on the occupier—seeing suicide bombing as a rational, strategic response to the perception that a foreign power has taken control of one's homeland—is a step forward, analytically speaking. The desire to regain control over territory does motivate some suicide bombers, accounts for the timing of some of their attacks, and sometimes results in concessions on the part of occupying forces. For example, my impression is that rational, strategic considerations linked to the desire to regain territory were more evident in the suicide bombings that took place in Israel, the West Bank, and Gaza between 1993 and 1997, and have been more evident in Iraq between 2003 and the present, than they were during the second *intifada* (Brym, 2007).

My analysis of suicide bombings during the second *intifada* shows, however, that focusing on occupation as the sole or even the most important reason for suicide bombings can be an oversimplification of a complex social process. In most of the 138 cases I examined, rational, strategic considerations linked to the desire to regain control of territory did not account for observable patterns in the objectives, timing, and results of suicide attacks.

It seems most fruitful to base explanations for patterns of suicide bombing on the *interaction* between occupied people and occupying forces. When other tactics fail to bring about strongly desired results, an occupied people may engage in suicide attacks out of desperation. But a resolute occupier has the will and the means to retaliate, often violently. Israel, for example, has responded to suicide attacks by engaging in the widespread assassination of Palestinian activists. Israel's actions have provoked more suicide attacks and other forms of collective violence on the part of the Palestinians, who are just as resolute as the Israelis; and renewed Palestinian violence has typically resulted in still more Israeli repression. I conclude that patterns of collective violence, including suicide bombings, are not shaped by one side or the other in the conflict. They are governed by a deadly interaction—a lethal and escalating dialogue—between conflicting parties. Interpreting that dialogue is the sociologist's job.

An Escalating Dialogue

Steven Spielberg's 2005 film, *Munich,* recounts the events surrounding the massacre of 11 Israeli athletes at the 1972 Olympics by Palestinian militants. A squad of Israeli secret service agents is quickly given the green light to track down and assassinate the Palestinians who masterminded the massacre. After the squad's first few hits, a letter bomb sent to the Israeli embassy in London kills an Israeli official. Other letter bombs are found at Israeli embassies in Argentina, Austria, Belgium, Canada, the Congo, and France. "They're talking to us," one Israeli agent says to another when he learns about the letter bombs. "We are in dialogue now."

The violent dialogue to which the secret agent refers has been going on for more than a century—almost since the first Eastern

European Jews arrived in Palestine with the hope of establishing a Jewish homeland and Arabs objected to their presence. Periodically, each side in the conflict comes to the conclusion that an escalation in violence will finally silence the other side, but it never turns out that way. Instead, after a lull, renewed and more intense violence erupts.

The importance of each side's resolve cannot be underestimated in the perpetuation of the conflict. American and French troops abandoned Lebanon in 1983 after one suicide attack on each of their barracks. Spanish troops exited Iraq immediately after the Madrid train bombings in 2004. In these cases, relatively low resolve on the part of the perceived occupiers resulted in their making quick concessions to the attackers. In contrast, in the Israeli and Palestinian cases, the probability of serious concessions is low because the resolve on both sides is so high.

In the most recent phase of their battle over territory that both sides claim as their historical and religious birthright, one side was too weak to imagine a balance of power, so instead it concocted a scheme to achieve a balance of horror, justified by the idea that "a nation whose sons vie with each other for the sake of martyrdom does not know defeat" (quoted in Oliver and Steinberg, 2005: 61). The powerful side responded to martyrdom operations (as suicide bombings are called by Palestinian militants) in the way that most of its enraged population demanded—by teaching the other side a series of lessons it wouldn't soon forget. The weak side obliged by remembering well and avenging its losses with all the fury it could muster. Some of the thinkers in Israel's strategic planning offices recognized that murderous retribution is often counterproductive. They had to answer to their political bosses, however, who were in turn obliged to respond to public outrage by getting tough. Some of the Palestinian strategic thinkers in the warrens of Gaza City undoubtedly knew that Israel would not capitulate in response to suicide bombing. But they had to answer to their publics too, and so they often forsook the strict calculation of costs and benefits for political expediency and a culture of mutual destruction.

To call the deadly interaction between Palestinians and Israelis "rational" distorts the meaning of the word. There is nothing rational about suicide bombing provoking assassination and assassination provoking more suicide bombing or other forms of lethal violence such as rocket attacks. The interaction pushes both sides further from their ultimate objectives of peace and security and threatens both sides with more horrible forms of violence in the future.

The irrationality of the interaction between Palestinians and Israelis was driven home to me at the New York conference I mentioned at the beginning of Chapter 2. It was a conference on human rights. One of the speakers was Dr. Yoram Dinstein, Israel's foremost expert on human rights law. Dr. Dinstein took part in a spirited debate on the legality of the Israeli policy of assassinating Palestinian militants. He reminded his audience that Israel is at war with a terrorist enemy, and Duchess of Queensberry rules therefore don't apply. He also suggested that Israel's assassination policy lowers the danger of violent acts against Israel by defusing human "ticking bombs."

I spoke to Dr. Dinstein after his lecture. "Legal issues aside," I asked, "do you really think that Israel's policy of targeted killings is rational?" I proceeded to tell him about my research suggesting that the assassination of Palestinian militants provokes more suicide attacks and other forms of lethal violence. I also argued that assassinations help to radicalize Palestinians, making it easier to recruit a new, larger, more determined and more ruthless generation of militants. Finally I mentioned the collaborator problem. Assassinations require real-time information on the whereabouts of targets. A large network of Palestinian collaborators feeds this information to the Israeli security services. The existence of this network causes mistrust, conflict, and internal violence among Palestinians in the West Bank and Gaza. Such social chaos undermines the unity and stability of Palestinian society that is required if one wants a negotiating partner who can make binding, authoritative decisions (Gross, 2003). Maintaining a wide network of Palestinian collaborators helps the Israeli security services locate targets in real time, but it also helps to undermine whatever slight chance for peace remains in the region. I concluded that, regardless of their legal status, targeted killings are politically irrational; they are intended to stop violence but have the effect of perpetuating hostility.

Dr. Dinstein dismissed my claims with a wave of the hand. "So," I suggested, "you conclude that the Palestinians understand only power?" To which he replied, "Even that they don't understand." And he was right. If the Palestinians understood power, they would have capitulated long ago. Instead, the exercise of repressive power by Israel only deepens their resolve. Which raises an obvious question that the legions of legal and counterterrorist experts have been unable to answer: If the Palestinians don't respond to the use of repressive power as "reasonable" people ought to, what is the good of using it? And if Israelis don't make concessions as Robert Pape says they should, what is the good of launching suicide attacks against them?

Social Interaction

Max Weber, a founding father of sociology, defined **social action** as human behavior that is meaningful in the sense that it takes into account the behavior of others. From his point of view, one person may intervene in a situation, a second may deliberately refrain from intervention, and a third may passively acquiesce in the situation. But all three act socially if their behavior results from taking into account what others are likely to do. Tripping on a rock is not a social action, but failing to speak up for fear of punishment is (Weber, 1947: 88).

Social interaction is a dynamic sequence of social actions in which people (or entire categories of people) creatively react to each other. Social interaction is of such fundamental importance that without it, individuals would not be able to develop a sense of identity—an idea of who they are. Nor would mere social categories (such as the residents of a particular street) be able to crystallize into self-conscious social groups (such as a true neighborhood).

Individual and group identity formation is possible only because humans enjoy a highly developed capacity to empathize or "take the role of the other" (Mead, 1934). We develop a sense of who we are by interpreting the actions of others and imagining how they see us. All social interaction—including interaction that involves conflict—sharpens a person's identity. In fact, nothing makes people feel more a part of their nation than a good war (Coser, 1956: 87–103).

The capacity to take the role of the other is especially valuable in conflict situations because it increases the likelihood of conflict resolution. This is well illustrated by *The Fog of War*, which won the

2003 Oscar for best documentary film. The film surveys the life of Robert McNamara, Secretary of Defense during the Kennedy and Johnson administrations and architect of the Vietnam War. In the film, McNamara outlines 11 lessons that he learned over his years of public service. His lesson number one: empathize with your enemy.

McNamara was present in October 1962 when President Kennedy was ready to start a nuclear war with the Soviets if they didn't remove their missiles from Cuba. Kennedy believed that Khrushchev, the Soviet leader, would never negotiate a removal. But Tommy Thompson, former U.S. ambassador to Moscow, disagreed. Thompson knew Khrushchev personally and understood that he would back down from his belligerent position if presented with an option that would allow him to remove the missiles and still say to his hard-line generals that he had won the confrontation with the United States. "The important thing for Khrushchev," Thompson argued, "is to be able to say, 'I saved Cuba; I stopped the invasion.'" Thompson convinced Kennedy. Negotiations began and nuclear war was averted. "That's what I call empathy," McNamara observes. "We must try to put ourselves inside [the enemy's] skin and look at us through their eyes." Note that being empathetic does not mean having warm and fuzzy feelings about an enemy but understanding things from the enemy's perspective so a resolution can be designed that will enable the greatest gains and the fewest losses.

The great tragedy of the Israeli–Palestinian conflict is that it has been so bitter and protracted that the capacity of each side to empathize with the other has been deeply eroded. An increasingly large number of Israelis believe that the Palestinians want to destroy Israel as a Jewish state and an increasingly large number of Palestinians believe that the Israelis want to prevent the creation of a viable Palestinian state. Increasingly, Palestinians fail to appreciate the legitimate security needs of Israel and Israelis fail to appreciate the legitimate national ambitions of the Palestinians. No Nelson Mandela-like figure who can peacefully reconcile the warring parties has risen above the fray, and the United States has not recently shown much willingness to drag both sides to the negotiating table and use its political and economic might to compel them to hammer out a resolution. It is therefore unclear whether the impasse can be broken anytime soon.

CRITICAL THINKING EXERCISES

1. According to this chapter, what is the main condition needed for bringing an end to violent conflict? Do you agree or disagree? On what grounds? How relevant is this condition for bringing an end to conflict in general, whether between individuals, groups, or nations? Answer these questions in three pages.

2. *Paradise Now* is a film about Palestinian suicide bombers that was nominated for the 2005 Oscar for Best Foreign Film. In the movie, best friends decide to undertake a suicide mission. Rent and view the movie. In a page, explain why one friend decides to go through with the mission while the other doesn't. Imagine yourself in the place of each friend. In a page, explain why you would or would not act as they did.

4

Hurricane Katrina and the Myth of Natural Disasters

A RACIST PRESIDENT OR AN ACT OF GOD?

On September 2, 2005, the NBC television network broadcast a tele-thon in support of American Red Cross disaster relief efforts along the coast of the Gulf of Mexico. Hurricane Katrina, one of the largest hurricanes of its strength ever to reach the United States, had made landfall about 80 hours earlier. Large swaths of Louisiana, Mississippi, and Alabama lay flooded and in ruins. After Harry Connick, Jr., sang "Do You Know What It Means to Miss New Orleans?" comedian Mike Myers and rapper Kanye West took the floor. Myers faithfully followed the teleprompter and described the wretched state of New Orleans and its people. But West veered wildly off script. He damned the mass media for their portrayal of black people as looters, criticized the government for taking so long to arrive with aid, and concluded with the memorable sentence, "George Bush doesn't care about black people." Myers then asked viewers to "Please call . . ." but didn't get to finish his sentence. Someone in the NBC control room apparently figured out where West was headed and ordered the camera to turn away and cut to comedian Chris Tucker (Dyson, 2006: 26–27).

Two months later, hip hop star 50 Cent was interviewed by Contactmusic.com. "I don't know where that came from," he said, referring to Kanye West's televised outburst. "The New Orleans disaster was meant to happen. It was an act of God" ("50 Cent...," 2005).

The comments by Kanye West and 50 Cent received a lot of attention and provoked much debate over whether the disaster was the result of one man's alleged racism or nature's wrath. From a sociological point of view, however, neither rap star came close to understanding how it came about that a storm in the world's richest and most powerful country could kill 2,300 people, cause more than $100 billion in damage, seriously disrupt the supply of oil and natural gas to the nation, and force the eventual evacuation of 80 percent of New Orleans's population.[1] After all, the danger of such a storm was widely and precisely known years earlier. The Federal Emergency Management Agency (FEMA) issued a report in early 2001 saying that a hurricane striking New Orleans was one of the three most likely disasters to hit the United States (the others were a terrorist attack on New York City and a major earthquake in San Francisco). Since 2001, long, detailed, and, as Hurricane Katrina later proved, shockingly accurate articles had appeared in *Scientific American, Time, National Geographic Magazine, Popular Mechanics,* the *New York Times,* and the New Orleans *Times-Picayune* that made the results of research on the effect of a powerful hurricane hitting New Orleans available to the broad public and its political representatives (see, for example, "Washing Away...," 2002). Yet almost nothing was done to prepare for the inevitable.

Explaining this sociological mystery is the chief aim of this chapter. My explanation consists of two main parts. First, for centuries powerful and well-to-do people made economic and political decisions that placed New Orleans, and especially its poor black citizens,

---

1 In June 2005, the Gulf of Mexico was responsible for nearly 30 percent of U.S. oil production and 20 percent of US natural gas production (Energy Information Administration, 2005). In addition to 1,836 confirmed deaths due to Katrina as of mid-May 2006, experts estimate that roughly 500 Louisiana residents were swept away and will never be found or identified (Krupa, 2006).

at high risk of hurricane-related death. Second, for an equally long period, powerful and well-to-do people resisted charging the American government with responsibility for ensuring the welfare of the citizenry as a whole. As a result, relatively inexpensive measures that prevent hurricane-related deaths in other countries have not been implemented in the United States. Neither God nor one man should be held responsible for the decisions and neglect of entire social classes.[2]

THE DEVELOPMENT OF NEW ORLEANS

In 1840, New Orleans was the fourth most populous city in the United States, and until the 1920s it was the world center of jazz. On the eve of Hurricane Katrina, it was still an important port and tourist town with a metropolitan population of more than 1.3 million. And, of course, it had a reputation. Tennessee Williams's *A Streetcar Named Desire* branded New Orleans as sensual and decaying. John Kennedy Toole's *A Confederacy of Dunces* rendered it a magnet for loose screwballs. Anne Rice added to its mystery in *Interview with the Vampire*. Everyone knew it as a party town, home of the Mardi Gras, a place that gave the world gumbo and jambalaya, and the only city in North America with a major street named after a 90-proof liquor.

New Orleans is situated on the coast of the Gulf of Mexico (see Figure 4.1). Most of it lies below sea level—in some places, as much as 8 feet below. To the south, the Mississippi River flows past the city, through wetlands, and into the Gulf. To the north lies Lake Pontchartrain, the second-biggest saltwater lake in the United States and the largest lake in Louisiana (see Figure 4.2). Imagine half a dozen exuberant 8-year-olds splashing in a swimming pool on a hot summer afternoon. New Orleans is like a plastic soup bowl floating in the pool.

---

2 **Social class** is one of the most important concepts in sociology, and much controversy surrounds its definition. For my purposes it is sufficient to define social class as a position occupied by people in a hierarchy that is shaped by economic criteria including wealth.

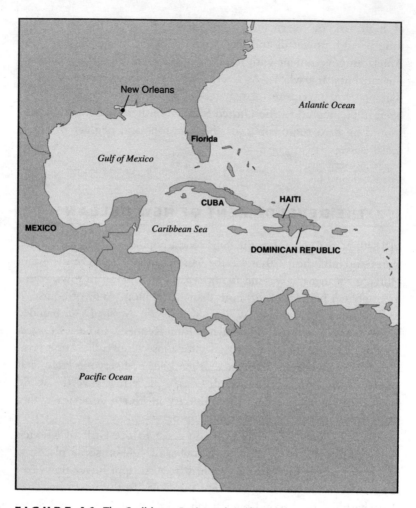

FIGURE 4.1 The Caribbean Basin and Gulf Coast
SOURCE: Adapted from U.S. Geological Survey (2006).

About 5 feet of rain falls on New Orleans annually—nearly 40 percent more than in New York. Every spring, the Mississippi tries to flood, and it often succeeded even after people started building dykes (or levees as they are called locally) to block the overflow. In the twentieth century, city residents achieved a measure of control over flooding by constructing a series of canals that allow 24 billion gallons

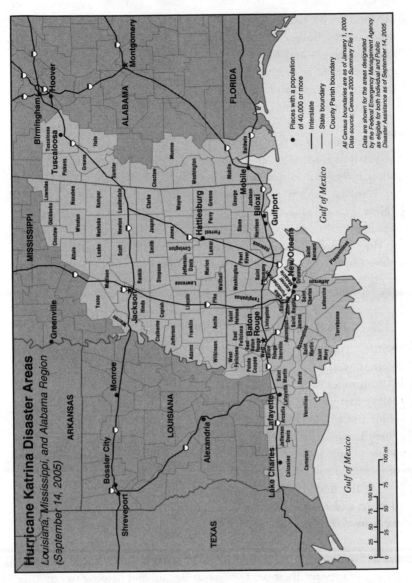

FIGURE 4.2 Hurricane Katrina Disaster Areas

SOURCE: U.S. Census Bureau (2005).

of water to be collected and pumped into Lake Pontchartrain and other nearby bodies of water every day. Still, every summer and fall, tropical storms and hurricanes assault the Gulf Coast. Sometimes, great waves of seawater surge into New Orleans. Levees were built to protect the city from storm surge, too (see Figure 4.3). Yet there is enough threatening water in the area to make a reasonable person ask why the French ever settled New Orleans in the first place.

They did so as part of their strategy for continental control. The Mississippi leads deep into the North American interior, links to other rivers that empty into the Great Lakes, and thus offers access to Canada, which the French had founded in 1608 (calling it "New France" [Sexton and Delehanty, 1993]). The swampy and treacherous Mississippi delta was difficult for the French to negotiate, so they settled 125 miles upstream from the river's mouth. Thus was New Orleans born in 1718. It served as one end of a continental bridge between French land holdings, a bridge that also served as a barrier to the westward drift of British settlers, who were already moving into the disputed Ohio River valley. Soon, several thousand French, Canadian, and German colonists, West African slaves, and Native Americans were living in New Orleans. Mainly because women were scarce, intermarriage was common, resulting in the formation of a distinct ethnic group, the Louisiana Creole, a social jambalaya that was unusually open to all races and cultures. With typical color and exaggeration, yet with a grain of truth, Louisiana Governor Huey Long said two centuries later that you could feed all the "pure" white people in New Orleans with half a cup of beans and half a cup of rice, and still have food left over.

In the middle of the eighteenth century, war broke out between Britain and France. France lost Canada, and its grip on Louisiana weakened. Spain took control of Louisiana for 38 years, and when the French resumed control they sold Louisiana to the United States for $15 million (about $400 billion in today's dollars), in one stroke raising money for their next war with Britain and helping to reinforce a power that could rival France's chief enemy.

White American settlers now flocked to New Orleans. Census data show that between 1810 and 1860, the population grew tenfold as the city became the country's second largest port. Tobacco, lumber, rice,

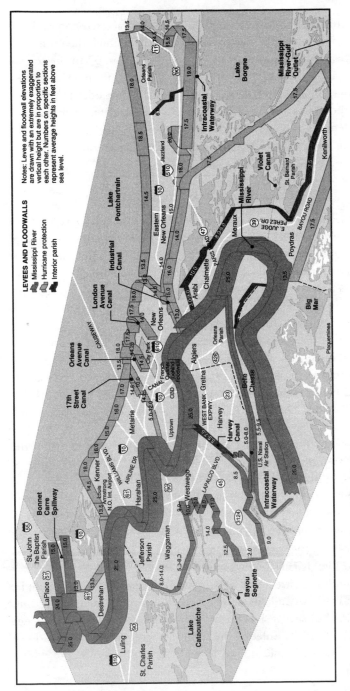

FIGURE 4.3 The New Orleans Levee System

sugar, cotton, and grain were shipped out. Manufactured goods, slaves, luxury goods, and coffee flowed in. In that half century, the number of New Orleanians of European origin increased from 37 to 85 percent of the population while those of African origin fell from 63 to 15 percent (Logsdon and Bell, 1992: 206). A distinct, modern American neighborhood was built uptown, its inhabitants separated from the Creole residents of the old French city by broad Canal Street and the Americans' sense of social, moral, and economic superiority.

The Growth of Black-White Inequality

New Orleans before the Louisiana Purchase was not a city without racial inequality. Black slaves were brought there from the beginning. Still, the color line was less rigid in New Orleans than in the cities of the United States. Racial intermarriage was relatively common. Many freed slaves lived in New Orleans, and they were often employed not as menial workers but as skilled tradespeople. French ideas about equality found eager supporters in the city. As a result, no sharp line separated blacks from whites. Social contact flourished among all categories of New Orleanians, fostered by musicians, live-in lovers, the Catholic clergy, grocers, and saloonkeepers. Class, culture, and complexion elevated many black residents to a status that most Americans of African descent could envy but not reach (Logsdon and Bell, 1992).

Once Americans started settling in the city, the situation of the black population deteriorated. In the 1840s and 1850s, an influx of white American workers displaced many freed slaves who had worked on the docks and in skilled trades. Racism increased as job competition mounted. Some freed slaves left for Haiti to escape it. Louisiana's fight to protect slavery during the Civil War (1861–1865) hardened the color line. Then, from 1890 to 1952, a series of laws institutionalized racial segregation. Blacks and whites now had to be kept apart in trains, schools, streetcars, bars, prisons, homes for elderly people, and even in circus audiences. They could not intermarry or cohabit, nor could they adopt a child of a different race. They could not dance or engage in athletic competition together. Blacks could not receive permits to build houses in white neighborhoods, and whites could not receive permits to build houses in black neighborhoods ("Jim Crow Laws...," 2006). A comparison of the situation before and after the Louisiana Purchase illustrates the fact that **races** are defined not so much by biological differences as by social forces. Specifically, racial distinctions are typically made and reinforced by advantaged people for the purpose of creating and maintaining a system of inequality.

In the 1920s, new levee construction permitted the shoreline of Lake Pontchartrain to be heightened and extended, creating desirable real estate north of the city for white residents (Hirsch and Logsdon, 1992). After World War II, new highways accelerated suburban growth. As a result of "white flight" to the suburbs, African Americans became a majority in the city of New Orleans proper after 1980, a position they had not held for 140 years. Just before Katrina hit, the city of New Orleans was 68 percent African American and just 25 percent non-Hispanic white. The poverty rate for African Americans was 35 percent—7.5 percent above the national average for African Americans. Two-thirds of the city's public schools were deemed "academically unacceptable" by the U.S. Department of Education. The city's homicide rate was the highest of any city in the country (Mahoney and Freeman, 2005). And the black population was increasingly concentrated in the city's least desirable, low-lying areas.

Flood Control?

The situation of New Orleanians was especially precarious because flood control measures were inadequate (Blumenthal, 2005; Bourne, 2004; Nordheimer, 2002; Tidwell, 2004). Two big problems existed:

1. *The disappearance of coastal wetlands.* When waves of seawater from the Gulf of Mexico are whipped up by hurricane-force winds, they pound New Orleans. The first line of defense against this onslaught consists of the marshes and barrier islands of the wetlands between New Orleans and the Gulf. Every 2 miles of wetland reduces storm surge by 6 inches. Before levees were built along the Mississippi, silt from the river's floodwaters used to stop or at least slow down the sinking of

coastal wetlands into the Gulf. But the levees divert silt into the Gulf, causing the wetlands to disappear at an alarming rate. The first line of defense against storm surge has thus been weakened.

In addition to removing much of the physical barrier against storm surge, the disappearance of the wetlands has another negative consequence for flood control. Hurricanes are machines fueled by heat. They gain strength from the heat that is released when vapor from warm seawater condenses and falls as rain. They weaken as they pass over land, which is cooler and, of course, drier. The disappearance of coastal wetlands has effectively brought the warm waters of the Gulf closer to New Orleans, ensuring that hurricanes have less chance to weaken before they make landfall.

2. *The inadequacy of the levees.* The second big flood control problem is that the levees along Lake Pontchartrain and in other areas around the city were last reinforced with higher walls after Hurricane Betsy struck in 1965, killing more than 70 people. The U.S. Army Corps of Engineers then built up the storm walls to withstand a category 3 storm.[3] Forty years after Betsy, the Lake Pontchartrain levees and other levees desperately required upgrading, as Hurricane Katrina painfully demonstrated. Katrina made landfall in Louisiana as a category 3 storm, and the surge off the lake smashed the levees, engulfing the city. In all, about half the levee system was damaged (Burdeau, 2006). What is worse, in any given year, New Orleans stands an estimated 1 percent chance of facing a category

---

3 The Saffir-Simpson scale ranks hurricanes as follows (National Weather Service, 2005):

- Category 1: minimum one-minute sustained winds of 74 to 95 mph and above-normal storm surge of 4 to 5 ft
- Category 2: minimum one-minute sustained winds of 96 to 110 mph and above-normal storm surge of 6 to 8 ft
- Category 3: minimum one-minute sustained winds of 111 to 130 mph and above-normal storm surge of 9 to 12 ft
- Category 4: minimum one-minute sustained winds of 131 to 155 mph and above-normal storm surge of 13 to 18 ft
- Category 5: minimum one-minute sustained winds greater than 155 mph and above-normal storm surge greater than 18 ft

Less than 17 hours before it made landfall in Louisiana, Katrina had been a category 5 storm.

5 hurricane. Allowing the levees to remain at less than category 3 readiness was like playing Russian roulette using an atom bomb instead of a bullet.

Aware of the problems just outlined, the federal government acted, but without resolve. It established a task force to help restore lost wetlands around New Orleans in 1990. In 2003, however, the Bush administration effectively ended that effort by allowing largely unrestricted development in the wetlands. Remarkably, in November 2005, two months *after* Katrina, the Bush administration refused to fund a $14 billion plan to restore the barrier islands and wetlands. (If that seems like a lot of money, bear in mind that it equals just six weeks of spending for the war in Iraq or 7 percent of the estimated cost of restoration following Katrina [Tidwell, 2005].)

In addition, Congress authorized a project to improve the pumping of water out of the New Orleans area in 1996. Unfortunately, the project was only half finished when money effectively dried up in 2003. The U.S. Army Corps of Engineers received money to improve the levees on Lake Pontchartrain and vicinity. But the Bush administration cut funding for the project by more than 80 percent in 2004 and made additional cuts at the beginning of 2005, ranking other priorities, such as the war in Iraq, higher. Because of budget cuts, the Corps was unable to buttress the 17th Street levee on Lake Pontchartrain, the location of the biggest levee breach during Katrina.

BREWING STORMS

New Orleans on the eve of Katrina was unusually poor, black, segregated, unequal, violent, and vulnerable to flooding. As we have seen, there was nothing natural about this state of affairs. Centuries of human effort—in the form of geopolitical rivalry, economic competition, public policy, and social exclusion—were required to create it.

People's actions may have contributed to New Orleans's vulnerability in another way, too. I refer to the increasing use of fossil fuels such as gasoline, oil, and coal. Burning fossil fuel releases carbon dioxide into the atmosphere. Carbon dioxide is a heat-trapping gas; it allows more heat to enter the atmosphere than escape it. The result is global warming. In turn, global warming may increase the intensity of tropical storms.

I say "may" because controversy surrounds the last part of my argument. Hardly any climate scientists doubt that the atmosphere is heating up or that the concentration of carbon dioxide and other heat-trapping gases has increased since the Industrial Revolution (Goddard Institute for Space Studies, 2006; Karl and Trenberth, 1999; Quaschning, 2003). A large majority of climate scientists believes there is a cause-and-effect relationship at work here, not a coincidence.[4] Leading scientific bodies in the United States, including the National Academy of Sciences, the American Meteorological Society, the American Geophysical Union, and the American Association for the Advancement of Science, agree that the evidence for human impact on climate is compelling. Few papers on climate change published in leading peer-reviewed scientific journals between 1993 and 2003 disagreed with the consensus view (Oreskes, 2004). In 2007, the report of the Intergovernmental Panel on Climate Change, which was written by 150 leading experts from more than 30 countries and reviewed by more than 600 scientific authorities, concluded that "human activities...are responsible for most of the warming observed over the past 50 years" (Intergovernmental Panel on Climate Change, 2007: 97). True, some scientists dispute the consensus. But their criticism should be taken with a grain of salt because much of their research is funded by the coal and petrochemical industries.

How might global warming affect hurricanes? In brief, global warming causes more water to evaporate. More vapor in the atmosphere may increase the frequency and intensity of hurricanes and cause the hurricane season to start earlier (Emanuel, 2005; Holland and Webster, 2007; Knutson and Tuleya, 2004; Webster, Holland,

---

4 More precisely, they believe that there is a cause-and-effect relationship with feedbacks that accelerate disequilibrium. For example, global warming melts permafrost. When permafrost melts, it releases methane, a much more potent heat-trapping gas than carbon dioxide. Global warming also melts the polar ice caps. When white ice is turned into dark ocean water, more solar radiation is absorbed by the earth and less is reflected back into space. Through these positive feedback loops, small temperature changes cause bigger temperature changes (Kolbert, 2006).

Curry, and Chang, 2005). Some scientists question whether enough data have yet been collected to substantiate these findings (Schiermeier, 2005a, 2005b). Therefore, the link between global warming and hurricane destructiveness must still be treated as a strong possibility rather than a proven fact. One thing can be said with certainty, however. If research substantiates the connection, it will be a global problem with deep local roots. With 4.6 percent of the world's population, the United States burns a quarter of the world's fossil fuels, more than any other country. And it is one of the very few countries that is not committed to substantially reducing their use.

A COMPARATIVE PERSPECTIVE

The strongest argument that deaths due to hurricanes are more a social than a natural disaster comes not from climate science but from sociology. It is an argument in three parts:

1. The populations of some countries are more exposed to the threat of hurricanes than the populations of other countries.

2. *At the same level of exposure,* some countries experience relatively few deaths due to hurricanes while others experience relatively many such deaths.

3. Countries that experience relatively few deaths take extensive precautions to avoid the catastrophic effects of hurricanes. Countries that experience relatively many deaths take few such precautions.

Figure 4.4 adds weight to this argument. The graph contains data from 34 countries that were exposed to hurricanes from 1980 to 2000. It plots the log of the number of people in each country who were exposed to hurricanes (along the horizontal axis) against the log of the average number of deaths due to hurricanes each year (along the vertical axis). In the period 1980–2000, the number of people exposed to hurricanes ranged from just over 18,000 in the small West African country of Cape Verde to more than 579 million in China. Average annual deaths due to hurricanes ranged from less than .5 in New Zealand to more than 7,400 in Bangladesh.

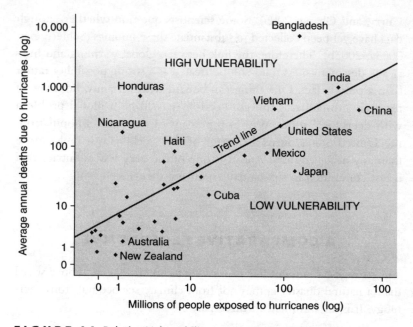

FIGURE 4.4 Relative Vulnerability to Hurricanes, 1980–2000

SOURCE: Compiled from data in United Nations (2004b: 38, 146). *A Global Report Reducing Disaster Risk: A Challenge for Development.* United Nations Development Programme. Bureau for Crisis Prevention and Recovery, www.undp.org/bcpr.

In general, countries with large exposed populations experienced more annual hurricane-related deaths than those with small exposed populations. That tendency is illustrated by the upward-sloping trend line. The line shows the number of deaths one would expect in an exposed population of a given size. Countries lying above the line were more vulnerable to hurricane-related deaths than one would expect given the size of their exposed population. Countries lying below the line were less vulnerable than one would expect given the size of their exposed population.

This is where the graph starts to get interesting. The exposed populations of Bangladesh and Japan were approximately the same size (126 million in Japan, 135 million in Bangladesh). Based on the size of their exposed populations, one would expect both countries to have experienced an average of about 250 hurricane-related deaths per year. Yet Japan experienced an average of only 39 hurricane-related deaths per year while Bangladesh experienced more than 7,400. That is partly because Japan took far more extensive precautions to guard against such deaths than Bangladesh did.

True, Bangladesh is one of the world's poorest countries while Japan is one of the richest. The Japanese can therefore afford to take precautions that the Bangladeshis can only dream of. But wealth is not the only factor that determines a country's ability to take precautions. After all, the United States is about as wealthy as Japan, had a considerably smaller exposed population (89 million people), yet it experienced an average of 222 hurricane-related deaths per year compared to Japan's 39. In fact, of the four rich countries represented in Figure 4.4, three of them—Japan, Australia, and New Zealand—experienced considerably fewer hurricane-related deaths than one would expect given the size of their exposed populations. But the fourth rich country—the United States—experienced about as many hurricane-related deaths per year as a relatively poor country with an exposed population of the same size. In the period 1980–2000, Americans were more vulnerable to death by hurricane than Mexicans (with 65 million exposed people and an average of 85 hurricane-related deaths per year) and much more vulnerable than Cubans (with 11 million exposed people and an average of just 3 hurricane-related deaths per year).

Cuba

The Cuban case illustrates well the kinds of precautions a country can take to prevent hurricane-related deaths, even if it is relatively poor (Cohn, 2005; Hamilton, de Valle, and Robles, 2005; Martin, 2005; Reuters News Agency, 2005; United Nations, 2004a). The last time Cuba suffered a large number of casualties because of a hurricane was 1963, when Hurricane Flora killed 1,126 people. After Flora, the Cubans took action to prevent a recurrence of the terrible tragedy.

They first implemented an educational program in schools, universities, and workplaces to teach people how to prepare for and cope with natural disasters. The program trains the population from a young age to interpret and heed weather reports, which are broadcast continuously and updated frequently in the event of an impending storm. Every May, an annual two-day training session known as Meteoro is held. It focuses on risk reduction, including exercises that simulate evacuation and rescue in the event of a hurricane. Meteoro also encourages preventative measures, such as trimming tree limbs and checking for weaknesses in dams, and it involves a review and update of all emergency plans in the light of what has been learned in the preceding year.

Cuba has organized its civil defense network to coordinate evacuation and rescue operations at the neighborhood level in the event of a big storm. Civil defense workers and members of organizations such as the Federation of Cuban Women go door-to-door to ensure that people fill their bathtubs with water, tape their windows, put their cars in the garage, unplug electrical appliances, and have an adequate supply of batteries, transistor radios, candles, matches, drinking water, and food. They create lists of the ill, elderly people, people with disabilities, and single mothers—people who would need help evacuating—and they ensure that help is available if these people are required to leave their homes.

If evacuation is necessary, neighborhood doctors evacuate together with residents so people who need medication can be properly treated. Refrigerators, TV sets, pets, and other valuable items are evacuated with the people so they won't be reluctant to leave. Evacuation routes, means of transportation, and temporary housing facilities for evacuees (mainly in schools) are set up well in advance, as are stores of emergency water, food, and medicine. The existence and locations of these stores are widely publicized. Buses, trucks, ambulances, vans, helicopters, even horse carts are mobilized to get people to shelter. Regular water supplies are turned off to avoid the spread of disease.

As a result of these precautions, Cuba lost only 22 lives in 10 major hurricanes between 1985 and 2004. But the big test for the Cuban system of preventing hurricane-related deaths came between July 7 and 9, 2005, when Hurricane Dennis, the most ferocious storm since Flora, lashed the island. Dennis hit Cuba twice as a category 4 storm (Katrina hit Louisiana once as a category 3 storm). One hundred and twenty thousand houses were badly damaged, 2.5 million people were left without electricity, and 30,000 acres of banana trees were flattened. However, the timely evacuation of 1.5 million people—a remarkable 13 percent of Cuba's population—minimized the loss of life. Dennis killed just 16 Cubans. One can very crudely estimate that if precautions similar to those employed in Cuba had been taken in the United States when Katrina hit nearly three months later, the American death toll would have been 128 people rather than 2,300.[5]

Cuba is a communist country. Some people might argue that its sterling achievement in preventing hurricane-related deaths has been accomplished only by means of strict political control of its population—control that freedom-loving Americans would never tolerate. But that argument is suspect. Vietnam is also a communist country with strict political control of its population, yet it is highly *vulnerable* to hurricane-related deaths (see Figure 4.4). Japan is a capitalist country *without* strict political control of its population, yet its record of preventing hurricane-related deaths is better than Cuba's. Communism versus capitalism is not the issue here. What is decisive in determining a country's tolerance of hurricane-related deaths is its population's collective will to take responsibility for helping fellow citizens in need, a will that is typically expressed through government policy. Compared to other rich countries, that collective will is weak in the United States.

KATRINA

Here is how it went down. On August 25, 2005, Hurricane Katrina hit Florida as a category 1 storm, killing seven people.[6] It then veered into the Gulf of Mexico, where it was soon upgraded to category 3. Kathleen Blanco, governor of Louisiana, declared a state of emergency

---

5 My logic is as follows: The United States is about 8 times more exposed to hurricanes than Cuba (89 million versus 11 million exposed people). There were 16 Cuban deaths due to Dennis, a storm of very roughly the same magnitude as Katrina. It follows that if the United States had taken precautions similar to Cuba's, Katrina would have killed approximately 128 Americans (since $16/11,000,000 = 128/89,000,000$).

6 The following account is based mainly on Dyson (2005), U.S. House of Representatives (2005), and reports in the *New York Times*.

on August 26 and President Bush followed suit the next day. New Orleans mayor Ray Nagin declared a voluntary evacuation order that night. At 10 a.m. on August 28, Nagin finally announced a mandatory evacuation order. At that point, Katrina was a category 4 storm about 20 hours from landfall. Seventeen hours later, at 3 a.m. on August 29, the 17th Street levee on Lake Pontchartrain collapsed. Other major levee breaches occurred at the London Avenue canal and the Industrial canal (see Figure 4.3). Eighty percent of New Orleans was soon flooded, in some places to a depth of 16 feet.

The response of the local, state, and federal government to the impending disaster was remarkably restrained, to put it politely. Top officials gravely underestimated the severity of the catastrophe about to befall residents of the Gulf Coast. Mayor Nagin hesitated to call a mandatory evacuation order because he was worried that the city would be legally liable for closing hotels, hospitals, and businesses. Consequently, he turned down an offer by Amtrak to evacuate several hundred New Orleanians on the last train out of town and he failed to mobilize the city's 804 operational buses to get people out. The Director of the National Hurricane Center had to call the mayor at home during dinner on the evening of August 27 to tell him that the storm was the worst he had ever seen and practically beg him to declare a mandatory evacuation order the next morning.

The White House found out about the 17th Street levee breach at midnight on August 29 but on the morning of August 30, President Bush, vacationing at his Texas ranch, expressed relief that New Orleans had "dodged the bullet." An e-mail confirming the levee breach had arrived at the Department of Homeland Security two-and-a-half hours before the information reached the White House, but the next morning, Michael Chertoff, Secretary of the Department of Homeland Security, flew to Atlanta for a conference on bird flu.

The consequences of official inability to appreciate the gravity of the problem were aggravated by woefully inadequate planning. For example, before the hurricane hit, nobody was in charge of overseeing the response and nobody had figured out how to avoid conflict over which agency should be in charge of law enforcement so that people could be evacuated effectively. The Louisiana transportation secretary was legally responsible for evacuating thousands of people from hospitals and nursing homes but had no plan in place to do so. The New Orleans Police Department unit responsible for the rescue effort was equipped with three small boats and no food, water, or extra fuel. For years it was known that 100,000 people lacked transportation out of the city. According to the 2000 census, residents of New Orleans were less likely to own cars than residents of any other city in the United States aside from New York, with its highly developed mass transportation system. Almost all of the New Orleans residents who did not own cars were black, poor, and/or elderly (Berube and Raphael, 2005). Yet an evacuation plan for these people was only 10 percent finished when Katrina struck.

Complicating matters further was the inexperience—many say incompetence—of high-ranking officials in the Federal Emergency Management Agency (FEMA). Five of the eight top people in FEMA, including its head, Michael Brown, joined the agency without any experience in disaster management. Many of the agency's top officials, including Brown, were political appointees whose chief claim to fame was loyal service during President Bush's run for the White House. Lacking professional qualifications and relevant job experience, such people often didn't know what to do and didn't appreciate how urgently they had to act. It hardly helped matters that FEMA had lost its independent status after becoming part of the newly-formed Department of Homeland Security in 2001 and then suffered budget cuts as resources were diverted to fighting terrorism. Little wonder that the New Orleans relief and rescue effort was slow, inadequate, and often brutal, leading to many deaths (see this chapter's Appendix).

Tens of thousands of New Orleanians were trapped in the flooded city after the storm passed. Many of them had to be rescued from rooftops by boat or helicopter. Moreover, the bowl was now overflowing with toxic soup; the waters that engulfed the city contained a witch's brew of industrial and household chemicals, sewage, garbage, and rotting human and animal corpses. People were nonetheless forced to wade through the waters to scrounge for drinking water, food, and medicine, and to get to higher ground. Conditions in the Superdome and the New Orleans Convention Center were especially appalling. Thousands of people sought shelter in those two buildings, where they were stranded for days in stifling heat, with little or no drinking water, food, medicine, or sanitation. Women miscarried, elderly people died; all suffered horribly (see this chapter's Appendix).

A Smaller, Whiter New Orleans

Many New Orleans residents returned home after Katrina. Five months after the storm, the city's population stood at two-thirds of its pre-Katrina level (Katz, Fellowes, and Mabanta, 2006: 5). Private insurance, individual spending, charitable contributions, and government aid have funded and will continue to fund clean-up, reconstruction, and levee repair and improvement. Progress has, however, been slow. In June 2007, 21 months after the storm, the city's population was still stuck at two-thirds of its pre-Katrina level (Jervis, 2007).

Class and race divisions were evident in the storm's immediate aftermath. Thus, some white New Orleans neighborhoods were extensively damaged by Katrina and some black districts escaped serious damage. Overall, however, a disproportionate amount of moderate and catastrophic damage took place in poor, black districts. Thus, if all residents returned to lightly damaged neighborhoods and none returned to moderately and catastrophically damaged districts, the city would lose 80 percent of its black population and 50 percent of its white population (Logan, 2006).

In the city's uptown district, life was in fact starting to return to normal just three weeks after the storm. Along its broad, tree-lined streets, work crews and hired help were restoring the Civil-War-era mansions, and well-to-do white families were already living in them. The uptown and other well-off districts (Algiers, the French Quarter, the Central Business District) are on higher ground and escaped the worst of the flooding. But the poor districts, where most of the city's African Americans lived, tended to be on low ground. There, flooding was typically more severe. Three weeks after Katrina, the poor districts were deserted. Much flood water remained, stagnant and toxic. Emaciated dogs were running wild. Everything was rotting (Mahoney and Freeman, 2005). Many of the houses in the poor districts had to be destroyed. Two years post-Katrina, after the Army Corps of Engineers had worked hard and spent a billion dollars to repair the city's hurricane protection system, prosperous neighbor-hoods like Lakeview had their flood risk from a big hurricane reduced by nearly five and a half feet. Poor neighborhoods like Gentilly had their risk reduced by just six inches (Schwartz, 2007).

It is unclear how many African Americans will return to New Orleans, but an indication of what might lie ahead comes from a sur-vey conducted in Houston between September 10 and 12, 2005, among 680 randomly selected Katrina evacuees. Ninety-eight percent of them came from New Orleans, 93 percent were black, and 86 per-cent had household incomes of less than $30,000 a year. Just 43 percent of the respondents said they planned to move back to their hometown ("Survey of Hurricane Katrina Evacuees," 2005).

African Americans are less likely to return than whites because they lack the money required to do so and, in any case, have less to return to. In addition, evidence suggests that reconstruction efforts discriminate against the black community. Such efforts have first con-centrated on less-damaged, white neighborhoods, delaying the recon-struction of predominantly black districts. As time passes and people get settled elsewhere, they are less likely to return. Most government grant assistance has gone to white, middle-class storm victims. In white districts, government loans to small business are approved at about seven times the rate of loan approval in poverty-stricken black neighborhoods. Blacks are less likely than whites to receive insurance settlements that will allow them to reconstruct their houses (Bullard, 2006). I conclude that the rebuilt New Orleans will likely be smaller and whiter than the pre-Katrina city. As has been the case throughout the history of New Orleans, class and race powerfully shape people's life-chances.

MARKETS, CITIZENSHIP, AND POWER

"I think you all know that I've always felt the nine most terrifying words in the English language are 'I'm from the government and I'm here to help.'"
—PRESIDENT RONALD REAGAN, 1986

Markets are social relations that regulate the exchange of goods and services. In a market, the prices of goods and services are established by how plentiful they are (supply) and how much they are wanted (demand). For example, if demand for labor increases and the supply of labor stays the same, the price of labor (the average hourly wage) rises. Workers spend and save more, and unemployment falls. In contrast, if the supply of labor increases and demand for labor stays the same, wages fall. Workers earn and spend less, and unemployment grows.

Late eighteenth-century Britain most closely resembled a completely free market for labor. However, the supply of labor exceeded demand to such a degree that starvation became widespread. The threat of social instability forced the government to establish a system of state-run "poorhouses" that provided minimal food and shelter for people without means (Polanyi, 1957).

Because perfectly free labor markets periodically cause much suffering and death if left unchecked, they must be regulated by governments. For example, North American laws outlaw child labor, stipulate maximum work hours, make certain holidays compulsory, and specify a minimum wage. Like most people, North Americans know that without such regulations, the whip of the labor market would destroy many of us.

The rights of people to protection under the law are embodied in the concept of **citizenship.** To varying degrees, citizens of different countries have fought for and won civil rights (free speech, freedom of worship, justice under the law), political rights (freedom to vote and run for office), and social rights (freedom to receive a minimum level of economic security and participate fully in social life) (Marshall, 1965). Note the phrase "to varying degrees." In the fight for citizenship rights, the citizens of some countries have been more successful than the citizens of other countries. And note the word "fight." Citizenship rights are rarely granted because of the grace and generosity of people in positions of power. They are typically extracted by subordinates using force. Consequently, success in achieving citizenship rights depends heavily on how powerful different categories of people are. **Power** is the ability to realize one's will, even against the resistance of others (Weber, 1946: 180). Oversimplifying for the sake of brevity, the balance of power between authorities and subordinates in a given society largely determines how extensive and entrenched citizenship rights become. If *subordinates* are relatively powerful, citizenship rights become extensive and well entrenched. Laws that ensure broad civil, political, and social rights are passed. Among rich countries, societies such as Sweden emerge in the extreme case. If *authorities* are relatively powerful, citizenship rights do not become extensive and well entrenched. Fewer and weaker laws ensuring civil, political, and social rights are passed. Among rich countries, societies like the United States emerge at the other extreme.

On almost every imaginable measure of citizenship rights, the United States lags behind the other 20 or so rich countries in the world. For example, long after all adult citizens won the right to vote in other rich countries, many African Americans were still unable to vote. It was only in the 1960s that African Americans won such rights. Nor did the United States lead with respect to women's voting rights. It became the twenty-sixth country to grant women the right to vote, following the Scandinavian countries, the British dominions, a number of continental European countries, and the Soviet Union. The United States compares unfavorably with other rich countries as far as social rights are concerned, too. Thus, the gap between rich and poor is greater in the United States than in any other rich country, and the proportion of the population classified as poor is larger. Americans enjoy no national health care system, no national system of paid parental leave, no national system of job retraining, and no national child care system. In recent decades, the government has slashed the number of families receiving welfare benefits and the cash and non-cash assistance available to each family. As a result, the plight of America's poor—disproportionately composed of children, single mothers with children, and African Americans—has been worsening steadily (Block, Korteweg, and Woodward, 2006).

According to former Harvard human rights professor Michael Ignatieff (now a member of Canada's parliament), the circumstances surrounding Hurricane Katrina demonstrate that the government of the United States has broken its "contract" with its citizens (Ignatieff, 2005). I disagree. The contract never stipulated that the American government would care much for its citizens in the first place. True, there have been periods when American governments were charged with greater responsibility. The Great Depression of the 1930s, with its massive nationwide strikes, and the civil rights era of the 1950s and 1960s, with its marches, demonstrations, sit-ins, and race riots, were times when Democratic administrations took important steps forward in that regard. But the overall tendency, grown stronger since Ronald Reagan first came to power in 1980, has been for government to minimize its involvement in the lives of its citizens, giving the freest possible reign to the forces of the free market. I conclude that the tragedy of Katrina was ultimately the result of the imbalance of power between upper and lower classes, and between authorities and subordinates, in the United States.

CRITICAL THINKING EXERCISES

1. Based on this chapter's analysis, list the ways in which natural disasters are influenced by human activity. Do you think that all types of natural disasters are influenced by human activity, or are some types of natural disasters relatively immune to human influence? Answer in one page.

2. This chapter argues that there is considerable variation from one country to the next in the relationship between state control and market forces. In a page, outline the conditions that might cause the relationship between state and market in the United States to become more like the relationship between state and market in Western Europe. In one page, explain why you think the likelihood of the United States becoming more like Western Europe in this regard is high, medium, or low.

3. A 2001 FEMA report listed the three most likely disasters to hit the United States: a major terrorist attack on New York City, a severe hurricane hitting New Orleans, and a serious earthquake shaking San Francisco. Based on what you learned in this chapter and what you can learn about the social structure of San Francisco on the web, write a five-page analysis of the likely effects of a serious earthquake shaking San Francisco. For recent

census data on San Francisco, visit http://factfinder.census.gov/ home/saff/main.html?_lang=en and search for San Francisco, California. For a detailed analysis of the losses that would be experienced today in the event of a repeat of the great San Francisco earthquake of 1906, read www.1906eqconf.org/ mediadocs/BigonestrikesReport.pdf. For a video on the 1906 quake, visit www.1906eqconf.org/ and select "Small Video" or "Large Video" below "View '06 The Next Great Quake Video."

APPENDIX TO CHAPTER 4

Written Testimony for the Record by Leah Hodges, Evacuee, New Orleans, Louisiana

Select Bipartisan Committee to Investigate the Preparation for and Response to Hurricane Katrina, December 6, 2005

I wish to thank everyone who is listening today for the chance to communicate my story. I come to Congress today representing not just myself, but hundreds, even thousands of other New Orleans residents who experienced the same or similar traumatic experiences and witnessed the same or similar events.

. . .

Let me begin with a few general points.

1. I don't need to point out the failures of the President, the Governor of Louisiana, and the Mayor of New Orleans, as these individuals have already claimed responsibility for everything that happened to us as the result of the hurricane and its aftermath.

2. The people of New Orleans were stranded in a flood and were allowed to die. The military had personnel stationed just 40 miles outside the city, and they could have moved in and gotten people out sooner. People were allowed to die.

3. Animals from the animal shelter and fish from the fish aquarium were evacuated before the people.

4. The President and local officials issued "shoot to kill orders" and people were shot. People who asked for help were threatened with being shot. My niece and her fiancé, they needed gas. Her fiancé asked [the] military [for] help and they told [him] "if you don't get back inside, we will shoot you."

5. Bodies are still being found every day in New Orleans. Most people in New Orleans do not believe the official body counts.

6. The devastation that hit New Orleans was foreseeable and avoidable, and because it was not avoided, New Orleans was turned into a mass grave.

7. As a hurricane survivor, I and my family were detained, not rescued.

My family was ordered to evacuate our home. We were directed to evacuation points. Beforehand, I, my mother, my brother, and two sisters visited a nursing home where the elderly clients had been abandoned by the owners and staff. There were five elderly persons there; the others had been evacuated earlier, perhaps by family. The day before the flood, the manager had come and told everyone they had to get out. Taking the keys to the bus that the home used to transport the senior citizens, the manager left them stranded. We rescued them. We shared all our food and provisions. When we approached the police and asked for help, they refused to help us. Instead, they threatened to shoot my baby brother.

We were then lured to the so-called evacuation points. This was several days after the hurricane had struck. The city was flooded. Soldiers had showed up with M16s and military weapons. They had declared New Orleans and Jefferson Parish a war zone. They loaded us onto military trucks after they told us they would take us to shelters where our basic needs would be met.

We were dropped off at a site where we were fenced in, and penned in with military vehicles. The armed military personnel brought in dogs. There, we were subjected to conditions only comparable to a concentration camp.

We were in a wide open space along the interstate and under the Highway 10 causeway. The overpass provided little shade, however. During the days, we were exposed to the hot sun. August is the hottest month in New Orleans. It was early September and still extremely hot. Our skin blistered. My mother's skin is still not fully healed.

We were just three miles from an airport, but we were detained there for several days. Many of those who were there when we arrived had already been there several days. On any given day there were at least 10,000 people in the camp. On my last day there, I would estimate there were still 3,000 detainees. By that time, nearly all the white people had been selected to evacuate first. They were put on buses and shipped out, leaving the remaining population 95 percent black.

There was muck and trash all over the causeway. Nothing was done to clean it up. At night, we were subject to sleep deprivation as low-flying helicopters were deliberately flown right over us. They would throw up the muck and trash, so that it would get all over us, even the pregnant women, the elderly, the infirm.

The military did not bring anything to help keep any of us alive. Not even a first aid kit. But they had body bags. They were doing nothing for the pregnant women. Some women miscarried. I know that conditions at the Convention Center were much the same. My niece was there. She was pregnant and she was terrified that her unborn baby had died. When she asked the military for help, they told her to wait until she was sure the baby was dead and then talk to them.

When I later spoke of my experience to a state trooper, he told me: "I would have rebelled." They set us up so that we would rebel, so that they could shoot us. At one point they brought in two truckloads of dogs and let the dogs out.

We would circulate through the camp to assist the sick and elderly and pregnant. One day, when I was on my way to get some water, I met a friend. He was a fellow musician. He told me that he wanted to try to get word out to the news media. But he was afraid to leave his family. I told him I would look after his family. But while he was gone I also had to circle back and check on my own family. I found that my brother had come up with an idea. He had persuaded a woman who was pregnant and due for labor to fake as if she were in labor. They told those in charge that she needed medical attention or she could have a miscarriage, and that got her out.

There was an old man from the senior center, he was an amputee. We had to carry him to the bathroom. They would not assist in caring for our people. The heat was unbearable. We got to the point we were so afraid of losing him to a heat stroke. We told them he was in a diabetic coma, that's how we got him out.

Mother is a cardiac patient, born with an enlarged heart. She suffers extreme hypertension. For three days I pleaded with them for care, and they would not do anything. Finally, on the third day, someone came out to check her blood pressure. The sphygmomanometer did not appear to be in working condition. I told the man, who was from the Coast Guard, to take my blood pressure first. The thing fell to pieces in his hands. It never worked.

The camp was so big, and people were scattered. People were deliberately kept apart. One woman was not allowed to see her two children.

At the camp, they lied and told us all the buses were going to the same place. They wouldn't tell us when the buses were coming. Meanwhile, my mother sat in the blazing hot sun . . .

On the last day they refused to give food and water to the ill for 24 hours.

People died in the camp. We saw the bodies lying there.

They were all about detention, as if it were Iraq, like we were foreigners and they were fighting a war. They implemented war-like conditions. They treated us worse than prisoners of war. Even prisoners of war have rights under the Geneva Convention.

5

✳

Sociology as a Vocation

IT'S ALL ABOUT THE CONTEXT

If this book has any value, then the next time you hear about people dying, you won't just ask, "What did they die of?" Instead, like a sociologist, you'll also ask, "What was the context of their death?" Analytically and practically, a world of difference separates the two questions. Consider that the four leading causes of death in the United States are heart disease, cancer, stroke, and chronic lung disease. Close to two-thirds of Americans die of these ailments. But the *context* in which these ailments become leading causes of death is one in which a quarter of the population is addicted to smoking tobacco and most people eat too much unhealthy food, get insufficient exercise, and are exposed to all manner of dangerous pollutants. Any analysis that focuses just on the immediate causes of death is inadequate because it fails to take into account the social context that allows heart disease, cancer, stroke, and chronic lung disease to become leading causes of death in the first place (Mokdad, Marks, Stroup, and Gerberding, 2004).

Focusing on context is important practically, not just analytically. Governments, businesses, charitable organizations, universities, and individuals invest enormous sums to increase life expectancy. Yet far more money is put into researching and coping with the immediate causes of death, such as finding cures for cancer, than solving contextual problems that give rise to the leading causes of death in the first place, such as reducing pollution and providing people with resources and incentives so they will eat healthier food, exercise more, and stop smoking tobacco. Few people doubt that we must continue investing heavily in research on the immediate causes of death. Not enough people understand that investing substantially more in solving contextual problems (if necessary, even diverting some funds from medical research) would let the average person live a longer, disease-free life. A dollar spent on prevention saves more lives than a dollar spent on treatment. Ignoring context—failing to think sociologically—kills people (Picard, 2006).[1]

Similarly, by investigating three social contexts in detail—the American inner city, the world of Palestinian suicide bombers, and the hurricane-prone Caribbean basin and the coast of the Gulf of Mexico—we learned much of practical importance for improving the quality of life and increasing life expectancy. We learned, first, that the defiant cry for identity known as hip hop has unfortunate consequences. Hip hop encourages deadly violence among some people. It also diverts attention from mobility strategies that are more likely than gangsterism to meet with success and thus improve the quality of life. We learned, second, that the policy of retaliation that is often involved in suicide bombings and targeted killings deepens the resolve of both sides in the Israeli-Palestinian conflict to kill each other. It thus moves both parties further away from a negotiated peace. And we learned, third, that the lack of disaster planning in some hurricane-prone regions greatly increases the chance that the most vulnerable members of society will perish. These lessons are sufficiently instructive that I feel wholly justified in claiming that sociology is a life or death issue.

But *caveat emptor*—let the buyer beware. I wouldn't feel comfortable selling you a bill of goods without telling you exactly what the purchase involves. Let me therefore close by offering a thumbnail

---

1 A century ago, the leading causes of death in North America were pneumonia, influenza, tuberculosis, and diarrhea and other intestinal ailments. From a historical point of view, the invention of antibiotics and increased life expectancy are also important contextual elements in the explanation of how we die.

sketch of how sociologists go about their business. That way, you can make an informed choice about how heavily, if at all, you want to buy into the discipline.

I can best describe what sociologists do by focusing on four terms: values, theory, research, and social policy. As you will now learn, sociologists' ideas about what is good and bad (their **values**) lead them to choose certain subjects for analysis and help them formulate tentative, testable explanations of the social phenomena that interest them (**theories**). Sociologists then systematically collect and analyze data to see if their tentative explanations are valid (**research**). Finally, based on the results of their research, they propose rules and regulations to govern the actions of organizations and governments in the hope of correcting social problems (**social policies**). Individual sociologists may specialize in theory construction, empirical research, or policy analysis, but the sociological enterprise as a whole involves all of these activities.

DOING SOCIOLOGY

Values

"There never has been, nor can there be, any human
search for truth without human emotions."
—VLADIMIR LENIN (1964: 260)

Someone once told Émile Durkheim that the facts contradicted one of his theories. "The facts," Durkheim replied, "are wrong" (quoted in Lukes, 1973: 52). Likewise, when a colleague's experimental evidence appeared to challenge his special theory of relativity, Albert Einstein's reaction was, essentially, "so much the worse for the facts" (Clark, 1971: 144). What's wrong with this picture? Aren't scientists' opinions supposed to be governed by respect for evidence? How then could a founding father of sociology and the greatest physicist of the twentieth century react in such a cavalier manner to facts that apparently falsified their views?

Actually, there is nothing wrong with this picture. Great scientists are human beings, and they can be as pig-headed as you and me.

Having invested so much time and energy developing pet theories, they may cling to them stubbornly even if evidence suggests that they are wrong. What is intriguing is that, despite such common human failings as obstinacy, vanity, short-sightedness, and narrow-mindedness, scientists routinely arrive at knowledge that is widely considered valid.

They are able to do so because people have designed the *institution* of science to eliminate ideas that can't be supported by evidence. The norms of science require that scientists publicize their findings and their methods of discovery, and that other scientists (with their own pet theories, prejudices, and professional rivalries) carefully scrutinize the work of their colleagues. Science is not quite a blood sport, but it does stimulate a lot of conflict over the validity of ideas and is therefore not recommended for the faint of heart. Out of this conflict there typically emerges a temporary consensus about what constitutes valid knowledge. A higher level of consensus exists in physics than in sociology, but in all disciplines it is the community of scholars playing by the rules of the scientific game that determines the prevailing consensus.[2] You don't get special consideration if you're a Durkheim or an Einstein. Consensus, not authority, rules.

I would not, however, want to leave you with the impression that scientists' values are always a danger to science. To the contrary, values are critically important in the scientific enterprise. They first play a role in determining what we want to study. As Max Weber wrote, we choose to study "only those segments of reality which have become significant to us because of their value-relevance" (Weber, 1964: 76). Values also fire our imagination and our intuition. They shape our ideas about how the parts of society fit together, what the ideal society should look like, which actions and policies are needed to help us reach that ideal, and which theories offer the best explanations for the phenomena that interest us (Edel, 1965). True, when values infuse science they may lead to subjectivity or bias of one sort or another. But

---

2 Because the rewards for innovation are many and scientists are only human, some of them are tempted to break the rules. They may falsify data, for example. But unlike ordinary criminals, who are sometimes able to conceal their illicit activities, scientists work in the open. As a result, the scrutiny of the scientific community almost always ensures that the rule-breakers get caught, usually sooner rather than later.

that matters little as long as scientists allow their peers to judge the worth of their ideas and form a binding consensus—and as long as outside forces such as governments and corporations don't interfere with their ability to do so. The scientific community's consensus is precisely what is meant by objectivity, and as long as consensus is allowed to crystallize and prevail, bias will be minimized. Thus, values are an important source of scientific creativity. They become problematic only if the scientific community fails to remain vigilant in its scrutiny of theory construction, empirical research, and policy proposals.

Theory and Research

"Practice should always be based upon a sound knowledge of theory.... Without it nothing can be done well...."
—LEONARDO DA VINCI (1956: 910)

As noted earlier, sociological theories are tentative, testable explanations of some aspect of social life. They state how and why certain social facts are related. For example, in his theory of suicide, Durkheim related facts about suicide rates to facts about social solidarity. Doing so allowed him to explain suicide as a function of social solidarity (see Chapter 1).

Non-testable explanations aren't scientifically useful. Some people believe that wealthy, unknown conspirators manipulate the price of gold and benefit from the price swings. Others believe that their physical ailments are caused by space aliens who routinely abduct them. Such theories are unscientific because they are not testable. Nobody has so far been able to observe, count, analyze, and interpret data that would allow us to decide whether they are valid. Note also that because scientific theories are testable, they are only tentative explanations. Research may disprove them at any time.

A theory may be little more than a hunch drawn from the experience of everyday life (Einstein, 1954: 270). But without some conjecture as to how facts are related, it is impossible to conduct meaningful research. That is what Leonardo da Vinci meant when he said that people cannot do anything well if they engage in practice (research and action based on that research) without theory. Starting research before developing a clear theoretical statement of how the relevant social facts might be related is a recipe for wasting years collecting and analyzing

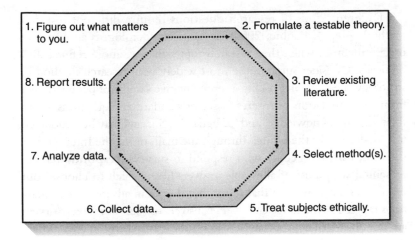

1. Figure out what matters to you.

2. Formulate a testable theory.

8. Report results.

3. Review existing literature.

7. Analyze data.

4. Select method(s).

6. Collect data.

5. Treat subjects ethically.

FIGURE 5.1 The Research Process

data in the field, the archives, or at a computer terminal. The reverse is also problematic. Theorizing without research is about as useful to science as exercise without movement is useful to the human body. From the comfort of an armchair, one can entertain the wildest of conjectures. The reality check known as research brings theorists down to earth and turns speculation into knowledge.

A stylized version of the sociological research process is presented as Figure 5.1.[3] As you already know, research can begin only when sociologists identify topics that they find significant (step 1) and hypothesize how observable facts central to their topic are related (step 2). Their next task is to review the existing theoretical and research literature (step 3). Reading previous work on the topic of interest stimulates one's sociological imagination and refines one's thinking. Besides, there is no point in rediscovering what earlier researchers have already found. Reviewing the relevant theoretical and research literature is an indispensable means of avoiding duplication of effort and learning from past insights, discoveries, and mistakes.

---

3 I say "stylized" because research is typically less orderly than Figure 5.1 makes it appear. For example, researchers usually jump back and forth between stage 2 ("formulate a testable theory") and stage 7 ("analyze data") many times before proceeding to stage 8 ("report results").

Different kinds of research questions require different research methods (step 4; Babbie, 2004). In general, sociologists adopt more precise methods when they research topics that are more refined theoretically. Consider surveys, the most widely used research method in sociology. They involve asking a representative sample of people drawn from the population of interest a set of standardized questions about their attitudes, knowledge, and/or behavior. Surveys may be conducted face-to-face, over the phone, through the mail, or via the Internet. For the most part, the people who respond to surveys (**respondents**) are presented with a list of allowable answers from which to choose. But insofar as surveys require that researchers know in advance what questions to ask and the range of possible answers to their questions, surveys are not always an appropriate research tool. Particularly in areas where theory is not highly developed—in **exploratory research**—it usually makes sense to conduct interviews that are less structured and more open-ended. This means that the interviews don't define a range of allowable responses. They do allow the spontaneous introduction of new questions whose importance emerges only in the course of the interview. In many cases, even conducting formal interviews is jumping the gun. For research in which theory is poorly developed and researchers have only a hunch about how observable facts may be related, one or another form of field research is often the method of choice. For example, **participant observation** involves spending considerable time in the social setting of the people who interest the researchers. It allows researchers not just to step back and observe their subjects' milieu from an outsider's point of view but also to step in and develop an understanding of the meaning people attach to the elements that populate their social world. From such observations, researchers may develop theoretical formulations that will permit more refined testing of ideas by means of structured interviews and surveys.

Many sociologists regard experiments as too artificial to provide valid knowledge about most forms of social behavior because they remove people from their social settings (recall our discussion of experiments on the effects of media violence in Chapter 2). As a result, the use of experiments in sociology is probably less widespread now than it was a few decades ago. In contrast, various methods that use historical records and existing documents as data are increasingly popular. For instance, sociologists have interpreted published histories to develop important theories about the uneven spread of industrial capitalism around the world and the turn of some countries to democracy, others to authoritarianism (Moore, 1967; Wallerstein, 1974–1989).

Once they leave their offices and begin collecting data, researchers must keep in mind four ethical commandments (step 5):

1. *Respect your subjects' right to safety.* Do your subjects no harm and, in particular, give them the right to decide whether and how they can be studied.

2. *Respect your subjects' right to informed consent.* Tell subjects how the information they supply will be used and allow them to judge the degree of personal risk involved in supplying it.

3. *Respect your subjects' right to privacy.* Allow subjects the right to decide whether and how the information they supply may be revealed to the public.

4. *Respect your subjects' right to confidentiality.* Refrain from using information in a way that allows it to be traced to a particular subject.

Ethical considerations are not restricted to the data collection phase of research (step 6). They come to the fore during the data analysis and reporting phases too. Hence two more commandments:

5. *Do not falsify data.* Report findings as they are, not as you would like them to be.

6. *Do not plagiarize.* Explicitly identify, credit, and reference authors when making use of their written work in any form, including web postings.

If theories propose conjectures about the way certain social facts are related, data analysis involves determining the degree to which the information at one's disposal conforms to the conjectures (step 7). Information can often be usefully turned into numbers. For example, if the allowable responses to a survey question are "strongly disagree," "disagree," "neither disagree nor agree," "agree," and "strongly agree," the responses can be assigned the numbers 1 through 5, respectively.

The advantage of turning information into numbers is that it permits statistical analysis using computers.

You can appreciate why computer-assisted statistical analysis is useful by imagining a spreadsheet with 240,000 cells. Since it is not unusual for surveys to ask 1,200 respondents 200 questions each, data matrices of this size are common in sociology (1,200 × 200 = 240,000). Each of the spreadsheet's 1,200 (horizontal) rows is reserved for an individual respondent. Each of its 200 (vertical) columns is reserved for responses to one question in the survey. That is a vast amount of information. Human beings don't have the ability to scan, unaided, a spreadsheet with nearly a quarter of a million cells and spot patterns in the numbers that would lead them to conclude that the data conform more or less closely to their theoretical conjectures. Computer-assisted statistical analysis is simply a means of finding patterns in the data matrix—patterns that allow one to see whether one's conjectures hold up. In milliseconds, an ordinary PC equipped with the right software can add up a column of 1,200 numbers corresponding to one opinion question in a survey and then divide the sum by the number of respondents who answered the question, telling you the average opinion of the respondents. Or it can compute a statistic that tells you how responses to one opinion question vary with responses to another opinion question, so you can learn how, if at all, the opinions are related. More complex statistical analyses showing, say, the unique and combined effects of class, race, gender, religion, place of residence, and age on political preference might take a few more milliseconds. The point is that having such pattern-finding power at one's disposal increases the researcher's capacity to test, reformulate, and retest theories quickly and creatively.

The final stage in the research process involves publishing the results of one's analysis in a report, journal, or book (step 8). Doing so allows other sociologists to pore over the research so that errors can be corrected and better questions can be formulated for future research. It also allows people to apply research findings to social policy.

Some sociological research is conducted with particular policy aims in mind and therefore has a direct impact on the formulation of rules, regulations, laws, and programs by organizations and governments. Most sociological research, however, has only an indirect impact on social policy. For example, no organization or government hired me to write this book, and I entertain no illusion that officials will read it and suddenly decide they need to change the way they do business. Like many sociologists, my aim is to influence the educated public and, in particular, young adults. I hope that my work will contribute, however slightly, to enlightening people about the opportunities and constraints that help shape their thoughts and actions, and assist them in making personal, organizational, and political decisions that will allow them and their fellow citizens to live happier and longer lives than would otherwise be possible. It's an immodest hope but, I think, not entirely unrealistic.

CAREERS

What about your hopes? Might they include the study of sociology? To make an informed decision on such an important issue, you need information on what you can expect from a sociology degree. You can get that by examining the careers pursued by sociology graduates. About 1.35 million Americans graduate with a bachelor's degree every year. Roughly 26,000 of them major in sociology. Some 1,900 will eventually receive a sociology MA, and 590 will earn a sociology PhD (estimated from National Center for Education Statistics, 2004, 2005).[4] What do they do with their degrees?

Most people with a *graduate* degree in sociology teach and conduct research in colleges and universities. Research is a bigger part of the job in more prestigious institutions. In 2003, average annual earnings stood at about $38,000 for all occupations, $49,000 for all white-collar occupations, $67,000 for all college and university professors, and $68,000 for sociology professors alone (U.S. Department of Labor, 2004: 73–74).

---

4 These estimates are based on U.S. data for graduates in the academic year 2002–2003. I assumed that the ratio of master's to bachelor's graduates and the ratio of doctoral to bachelor's graduates in 2002–2003 are equal to the proportion of bachelor's students who eventually graduate with MAs and PhDs.

Many sociologists with a graduate degree conduct research and give policy advice in institutions outside the system of higher education. The number of research and policy-related jobs for sociologists is growing faster than the number of teaching jobs. In government, sociologists help formulate research-based policy in such areas as health, social welfare, economic and social development, the elderly, youth, criminal justice, science, and housing (House, 2005). Nongovernmental agencies that employ sociologists include professional and public-interest associations and trade unions. In the private sector, sociologists practice their craft in firms that specialize in public opinion polling, management consulting, market research, standardized testing, and evaluation research, which assesses the impact of policies and programs.

An *undergraduate* major in sociology is excellent preparation for many fields other than sociology (Stephens, 1998). Recent research shows that about 40 percent of people who major in sociology intend to go to graduate or professional school. Of those who aspire to do so, more than 82 percent expect to choose fields other than sociology (Spalter-Roth, Erskine, Polsiak, and Panzarella, 2005: 24–25). Their top choices are listed below in order of popularity:

1. education
2. counseling/psychology
3. applied sociology (MA)
4. social work
5. law
6. criminology
7. sociology (PhD)
8. medicine/nursing
9. marketing/business administration
10. public affairs/public policy
11. communication

With respect to the job market, the value of a sociology major lies partly in the generic skills it offers rather than any specifically technical skills associated with it (Davies and Walters, 2007). Sociology majors (as well as majors in the other social sciences) tend to be adept in interpersonal relations, communication, decision making, critical thinking, conflict management, the assumption of authority, and the application of abstract ideas to real-life situations. As a result, they can be trained quickly and effectively to do any number of jobs in the quickly growing service sector of the economy. Most employers are aware of the utility of these skills. Consequently, one Canadian study found that the unemployment rate was lower among social science graduates than among science graduates and that there were more new jobs available for people with social science degrees than for people with degrees in other fields. As a bonus, the discrepancy between men's and women's incomes was smallest among social science graduates (Allen, 1999).

POSITIVE AND NEGATIVE FREEDOM

Now that I have sketched what sociologists do and how you might fit into the sociological enterprise, there remains the task of summarizing the values, theories, and policies that I have introduced in this book.

Underlying my analyses is a particular conception of human **freedom** that I have come to value highly and that I must first clarify.

Political philosophers distinguish negative freedom from positive freedom (Berlin, 2002b; MacCallum, 1967). **Negative freedom** is freedom *from* constraints that would otherwise prevent me from doing as I wish. When I have the right to vote, express my opinions publicly, and associate with whomever I wish, I enjoy negative freedom. That is because I can engage in these activities only when nobody prevents me from doing so. Note that non-interference from the state is usually required if I am to enjoy negative freedom.

In contrast, **positive freedom** is the capacity *to* act rationally. It involves taking control of one's life and realizing one's best interests. When I receive a higher education and good medical treatment in the event of ill health, I enjoy positive freedom. That is because I require such benefits if I am to realize my best interests. However, because particular individuals may be incapable of understanding their best interests, it is typically necessary for some higher authority, such as the state, to help define those interests and provide the benefits needed to attain them.

Some political philosophers argue that positive freedom and negative freedom are incompatible. If you have more positive freedom, they say, you must have less negative freedom, and vice versa. The notion that positive and negative freedoms are rivals was first proposed by Sir Isaiah Berlin in the mid-twentieth century (Berlin, 2002b). Berlin argued that if the state tried to define the best interests of the citizenry and provide the benefits it deemed necessary to attain them, it could easily slip into authoritarianism. He pointed to the Soviet Union as a case in point. The rulers of the Soviet Union, guided by communist ideology, claimed to know what was required for the citizenry to realize its best interests. The state provided free education, child care, medical care, and so on, but people were not free to vote for the party of their choice, openly practice their religion, express their opinions publicly, or associate with whomever they chose.

In contrast to Berlin's argument, this book is based on the idea that positive and negative freedom *are* generally compatible (Taylor, 1985). Figure 5.2 supports the validity of my claim. It contains data on all 123 countries for which recent data on positive and negative freedom exist. It plots an index of negative freedom (along the horizontal axis) against an index of positive freedom (along the vertical axis). The index of negative freedom combines information on freedom to vote, freedom of the press, freedom of assembly, and other political and civil liberties in each country. It indicates the degree to which people are free from state oppression. The index of positive freedom combines information on average level of education, adult literacy, and life expectancy in each country. It indicates the degree to which people are free to realize their interests because they have the state support (through education and health care) to do so. If Berlin's argument held, we would expect to discover an inverse relationship between positive and negative freedom—the more of one, the less of the other. But the trend line in Figure 5.2 shows just the opposite. The countries ranking highest on positive freedom also tend to rank highest on negative freedom. The countries ranking lowest on positive freedom also tend to rank lowest on negative freedom. Some countries deviate from this tendency, but the overall association between positive

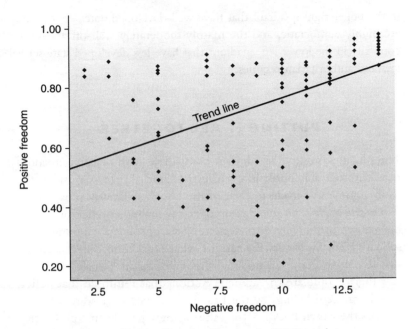

FIGURE 5.2 Positive by Negative Freedom in 123 Countries

Note: Data are for the latest year available. Negative freedom is measured by the index of political and civil liberties, which is calculated annually by Freedom House, a nonpartisan organization that promotes democracy around the world. Positive freedom is measured by life expectancy at birth, the literacy rate for people over the age of 14, and enrollment ratios at all levels of education, as calculated annually by United Nations social scientists.

SOURCE: Compiled from Freedom House (2006); United Nations (2005: 219–22).

and negative freedom is moderately strong.[5] In general, then, and contrary to what Berlin argued, negative and positive freedoms are usually not rivals. In most cases, states that intervene to provide benefits to the citizenry also *remove* political constraints from their citizens. States that constrain their citizens the most tend to provide *fewest* benefits to the citizenry. What gives the trend line in Figure 5.2 its upward slope are the mainly rich and moderately well-off countries

---

5 The **correlation coefficient** (*r*) measures the degree of association between variables. It ranges in value from –1 (a perfect inverse correlation, in which a unit increase in one variable is associated with a unit decrease in the other variable) to +1 (a perfect positive correlation, in which a unit increase in one variable is associated with a unit increase in the other variable). An *r* of 0 indicates no correlation between two variables. For the two variables arrayed in Figure 5.2, *r* = 0.486, which indicates a moderately strong positive correlation.

in the upper right quadrant that have well-developed state services and are highly democratic, and the mainly moderately well-off and poor countries in the lower left quadrant that have less developed state services and authoritarian regimes.

PUTTING IT ALL TOGETHER

The idea that positive freedom is compatible with negative freedom runs through this book like a multicolored thread. Consider the main arguments I made in each of the book's substantive chapters.

In the chapter on suicide bombers, my main theoretical argument boils down to the view that decreasing social solidarity among high-solidarity groups lowers the rate of what Durkheim called altruistic suicide. With good reason, militant Palestinians believe that they and their people are threatened. Actions that reinforce that belief, such as targeted killings by the Israeli state, encourage some of them to take their own lives for the sake of their people. It follows that decreasing the perceived threat will lower social solidarity and the frequency of suicide attacks. I suggested specific state actions to achieve that end: the elimination of targeted killings by Israel and the use of powerful diplomatic and economic levers by the United States to compel both sides to negotiate a settlement that recognizes their territorial and security needs. The positive freedom to live in peace requires such brave and energetic state intervention, in my view. I believe, moreover, that, absent their chronic conflict, Palestinians and Israelis would be able to remove restrictions on political and civil liberties that now constrain people in both societies. Peace would also allow negative freedom to grow in the Middle East.

The main theoretical argument of the chapter on the myth of natural disasters is that when the state provides higher standards of security and well-being to the most vulnerable members of society, it increases their welfare and lowers their chance of death due to natural disasters. At the risk of raising a red flag, so to speak, I made the point by comparing the treatment of vulnerable populations in the United States and Cuba. I fully appreciate that some readers will react negatively to my suggestion that the United States can learn a valuable lesson from a communist country. That is why I emphasized that Japan, too, takes exactly the measures that I think are necessary to protect vulnerable citizens without restricting anyone's negative freedom. The Japanese case demonstrates that freedom from excessive state authority and the freedom of society's most vulnerable members to live in relative safety can coexist.

Finally, in the chapter on hip hop, we visited the American inner city, where the sense of community is weak and social institutions, especially families and schools, are crumbling. As Durkheim would lead us to expect in such an anomic social setting, the rate of suicide among inner-city black youth is high and rising quickly. Other forms of violence leading to death, notably homicide, also proliferate, as do cultural products such as hip hop that sometimes glorify violence. Again, I claimed that state intervention could help shore up and provide alternatives to faltering social institutions. More engaging and higher-quality schools, widely accessible child care programs, and organized after-school athletic activities would, for example, make the inner city less anomic. Gun control—especially the banning of handguns and automatic assault rifles—would also help. Such policies would increase the positive freedom of residents in the inner city to live more secure lives and enjoy better prospects for upward mobility. They would also increase negative freedom by lowering the constraints on life imposed by coercive violence.

Such are my arguments. I do not ask you to agree with them. I do invite you to engage in a debate with your fellow students and professors on the subjects I have raised, using logic, evidence, and the sociological perspective to add substance to your views. As you do so, you may discover, as I did when I was 19, that sociology is not just a course but a calling.

CRITICAL THINKING EXERCISES

1. In one page, outline the roles of subjectivity and objectivity in scientific research.

2. In one page, explain the relationship between values, theory, research, and social policy.

3. In one page, explain the relationship between negative freedom and positive freedom.

Glossary

Absolute deprivation Long-standing poverty and unemployment.

Altruistic suicide *See* **Suicide**.

Anomic suicide *See* **Suicide**.

Citizenship Rights of people to various protections under the law. Specifically, and to varying degrees, citizens of different countries have fought for and won civil rights (free speech, freedom of religious choice, justice under the law), political rights (freedom to vote and run for office) and social rights (freedom to receive a minimum level of economic security and to participate fully in social life).

Correlation coefficient Measurement of the degree of association between variables. The correlation coefficient, r, ranges in value from -1 (a perfect inverse correlation, in which a unit increase in one variable is associated with a unit decrease in the other variable) to $+1$ (a perfect positive correlation, in which a unit increase in one variable is associated with a unit increase in the other variable). An r of 0 indicates no correlation between two variables.

Culture The sum total of shared and socially transmitted languages, beliefs, symbols, values, material objects, routine practices, and art forms that people create to help them survive and prosper.

Determinism The belief that everything happens the way it does because it was destined to happen in just that way.

Egoistic suicide *See* **Suicide**.

Experiments Carefully controlled artificial situations that allow researchers to isolate presumed causes and measure their effects precisely. Typically, subjects are randomly divided into experimental and control groups. Only the experimental group is exposed to the presumed cause. The hypothesized effect is measured in the experimental and control groups before and after exposure. By comparing the measures of the effect before and after exposure in both the experimental and control groups, experimenters can determine how much influence the presumed cause had on the hypothesized effect.

Exploratory research Systematic observation of people in their natural social settings that attempts to develop a theory about a social phenomenon with little or no previous research on the subject.

Field research Systematic observation of people in their natural social settings.

Freedom Freedom has negative and positive aspects. **Negative freedom** is the absence of constraint. It is freedom *from* obstacles that would otherwise prevent me from doing as I wish. **Positive freedom** is the capacity to take control of one's life and realize one's best interests. It is freedom *to* act rationally.

Homicide rate The number of murders per 100,000 people in a population.

Least-squares regression line (or trend line) A straight line in a two-dimensional graph that is drawn so as to minimize the sum of the squared perpendicular distances between each data point and the line itself.

Markets Social relations that regulate the exchange of goods and services. In a market, the prices of goods and services are established by how plentiful they are (supply) and how much they are wanted (demand).

Negative freedom *See* **Freedom**.

Official statistics Numerical data compiled by state organizations for purposes other than sociological research.

Participant observation A type of research that involves spending considerable time in the natural social setting of the people who interest the researcher, allowing the researcher not just to step back and observe his or her subjects' milieu from an outsider's point of view but also to step in and develop an understanding of the meaning people attach to the elements that populate their social world.

Population The entire group that a researcher wants to learn about.

Positive freedom *See* **Freedom**.

Power The ability to realize one's will, even against the resistance of others.

Races Categories of people defined not so much by biological differences as by social forces. Specifically, racial distinctions are typically made and reinforced by advantaged people for the purpose of creating and maintaining a system of inequality.

Rates Rates allow comparisons between groups of different size. To calculate the rate at which an event occurs, divide the number of times an event occurs by the total number of people to whom the event could occur in principle. Then calculate how many times it would occur in a population of standard size (say, 100,000).

Relative deprivation The growth of an intolerable gap between what people expect and what they get out of life.

Research The process of systematically collecting and analyzing data to test theories.

Respondents Members of a sample who respond to survey questions.

Sample The part of a group of interest that researchers study to learn about the group as a whole.

Sex ratio The number of men per 100 women in a population.

Social action Human behavior that is meaningful in the sense that it takes into account the behavior of others.

Social class Position occupied by people in a hierarchy that is shaped by economic criteria including wealth.

Social interaction Dynamic sequence of social actions in which people (or groups) creatively react to each other.

Social policy Rules and regulations that organizations and governments establish to correct social problems.

Social solidarity Social solidarity refers to (1) the degree to which group members share beliefs and values, and (2) the intensity and frequency of their interaction.

Social structures Relatively stable patterns of social relations that create opportunities for and constrain the way people think and act.

Sociology The systematic study of human behavior in social context.

Suicide Taking one's own life. Suicide may take several forms, according to Émile Durkheim. He called suicides that occur in high-solidarity settings **altruistic.** In contrast, suicides that occurs in low-solidarity settings are egoistic or anomic. **Egoistic suicide** results from a lack of integration of the individual into society because of weak social ties to others. **Anomic suicide** occurs when norms governing behavior are vaguely defined.

Survey Research method in which randomly selected people are asked standardized questions about their knowledge, attitudes, or behavior. Researchers aim to study part of a group (a sample) to learn about the whole group of interest (the population).

Theories Tentative, testable explanations of phenomena.

Upward mobility Movement upward within a system of inequality.

Values Ideas about what is good and bad.

Voluntarism Belief that people alone control their destiny.

References

Agenda Inc. 2006. "American Brandstand 2005." http://www.agendainc
.com/brandstand05.pdf (accessed March 27, 2006).

Allen, Robert C. 1999. *Education and Technological Revolutions: The Role of the Social Sciences and the Humanities in the Knowledge Based Economy.* Ottawa: Social Sciences and Humanities Research Council of Canada.

al-Quds (Jerusalem). 2000–2005. [Arabic: *Jerusalem.*]

al-Quds al-'Arabi (London) 2000–2005. [Arabic: *Arab Jerusalem.*]

"al-Ra'is: 'Amaliyat Nitanya Juramat did Sha'buna.'" [Arabic: "The President: 'Netanya Operation Is a Crime against Our People.'"] 2005. *al-Quds,* July 12: 1A.

American Society of Plastic Surgeons. 2006. "2005 Cosmetic Plastic Surgery Trends." http://www.plasticsurgery.org/public_education/ Statistical-Trends.cfm (accessed September 14, 2006).

Anderson, Craig, and Brad J. Bushman. 2002. "The Effects of Media Violence on Society." *Science* 295, 5564: 2377–79.

Anderson, Michael. 2003. "Reading Violence in Boys' Writing." *Language Arts* 80, 3: 223–31.

Appleby, John, Maxime Fougère, and Manon Rouleau. 2004. "Is Post-Secondary Education in Canada a Cost-Effective Proposition?" Applied Research Branch, Strategic Policy, Human Resources Development Canada. http://www11.hrsdc.gc.ca/en/cs/sp/hrsdc/arb/ publications/research/2002-000150/page01.shtml (accessed May 25, 2005).

Arian, Asher. 2001. "Israeli Public Opinion in the Wake of the 2000–2001 Intifada." *Strategic Assessment* 4: 2. http://www.tau.ac.il/jcss/sa/v4n2p.Ari.html (accessed May 15, 2005).

_____. 2002. "A Further Turn to the Right: Israeli Public Opinion on National Security—2002." *Strategic Assessment* 5: 1. http://www.tau.ac.il/jcss/sa/v5n1p4Ari.html (accessed May 15, 2005).

Associated Press. 2005. "Lil' Kim Sentenced to a Year in Prison." *MSNBC.com,* July 6. http://www.msnbc.msn.com/id/8485039/ (accessed April 20, 2006).

Atran, Scott. 2003. "Genesis of Suicide Terrorism." *Science* 299, 5612: 1534–39.

Babbie, Earl. 2004. *The Practice of Social Research,* 10th ed. Belmont, CA: Wadsworth.

Bayles, Martha. 1994. *Hole in Our Soul: The Loss of Beauty and Meaning in American Popular Music.* Chicago: University of Chicago Press.

Becker, Ernest. 1971. *The Birth and Death of Meaning: An Interdisciplinary Perspective on the Problem of Man.* New York: Free Press.

_____. 1973. *The Denial of Death.* New York: Free Press.

Berger, Peter L., and Thomas Luckmann. 1967. *The Social Construction of Reality: A Treatise in the Sociology of Knowledge.* Garden City, NY: Doubleday.

Berlin, Isaiah. 2002a. "Historical Inevitability." In Henry Hardy, ed., *Liberty* (pp. 94–165). Oxford, UK: Oxford University Press.

_____. 2002b. "Two Concepts of Liberty." In Henry Hardy, ed., *Liberty* (pp. 166–217). Oxford: Oxford University Press.

Berube, Alan, and Steven Raphael. 2005. "Access to Cars in New Orleans." The Brookings Institution. http://www.brookings.edu/metro/20050915_katrinacarstables.pdf (accessed May 30, 2006).

Block, Fred, Anna C. Korteweg, and Kerry Woodward. 2006. "The Compassion Gap in American Poverty Policy." *Contexts* 5, 2: 14–20.

Blumenthal, Sidney. 2005. "No One Can Say They Didn't See It Coming." *Salon.com,* August 31. http://dir.salon.com/story/opinion/blumenthal/2005/08/31/disaster_preparation/index_np.html (accessed May 31, 2006).

Bourne, Joel. K. 2004. "Gone with the Water." *National Geographic Magazine,* October. http://magma.nationalgeographic.com/ngm/0410/feature5/?fs=www3.nationalgeographic.com (accessed May 30, 2006).

Boyle, Brendan. 2006. "Thermopylae: Round One in the Clash of Civilizations." *New York Sun,* December 4. http://www2.nysun.com/article/44526 (accessed March 28, 2008).

Browne, Kevin D., and Catherine Hamilton-Giachritsis. 2005. "The Influence of Violent Media on Children and Adolescents: A Public-Health Approach." *The Lancet* 365, 9460: 702–10.

Brym, Robert J. 1983. "Israel in Lebanon." *Middle East Focus* 6, 1: 14–19.

_____. 2007. "Six Lessons of Suicide Bombers." *Contexts* 8, 4: 40–45.

_____. 2008. "Religion, Politics and Suicide Bombing: An Interpretative Essay." *Canadian Journal of Sociology* 33, 1. http://ejournals.library .ualberta.ca/index.php/CJS/article/view/1537/1061 (accessed March 28, 2008).

_____, and Bader Araj. 2006. "Suicide Bombing as Strategy and Interaction: The Case of the Second *Intifada*." *Social Forces* 84: 1965–82.

_____, and Bader Araj. Forthcoming 2008. "Palestinian Suicide Bombing Revisited: A Critique of the Outbidding Thesis." *Political Science Quarterly* 123, 3.

_____, and John Lie. 2007. *Sociology: Your Compass for a New World,* 3rd ed. Belmont, CA: Wadsworth.

Bullard, Robert D. 2006. "Katrina and the Second Disaster: A Twenty-Point Plan to Destroy Black New Orleans." http://www.ejrc.cau.edu/ Bullard20pointplan.html (accessed May 18, 2006).

Burdeau, Cain. 2006. "Corps of Engineers Takes Responsibility for New Orleans Flooding." *Associated Press Newswires,* June 1.

"The Celebrity 100." 2005. *Forbes.com,* June 15. http://www.forbes.com/ celebrity100/ (accessed March 27, 2006).

Clark, Ronald W. 1971. *Einstein: The Life and Times.* New York: Avon.

Cohn, Marjorie. 2005. "The Two Americas." *Truthout,* September 3. http://www.truthout.org/docs_2005/090305Y.shtml (accessed July 26, 2006).

Combs, Sean "Puffy," and the Lox. 1997. "I Got the Power." http:// www.ewsonline.com/badboy/lyrpow.html (accessed March 22, 2000).

Coser, Lewis. 1956. *The Functions of Social Conflict.* New York: Free Press.

Dale, Stephen Frederic. 1988. "Religious Suicide in Islamic Asia: Anticolonial Terrorism in India, Indonesia, and the Philippines." *Journal of Conflict Resolution* 32, 1: 37–59.

Davies, Scott, and David Walters. 2007. "The Value of a Sociology Degree." In Robert J. Brym, ed., *Society in Question,* 5th ed. (pp. 10–18). Toronto: Nelson.

Davis, Joyce M. 2003. *Martyrs: Innocence, Vengeance and Despair in the Middle East.* New York: Palgrave Macmillan.

Davis, Mike. 1990. *City of Quartz: Excavating the Future in Los Angeles.* New York: Verso.

da Vinci, Leonardo. 1956. "Of the Error Made by Those Who Practise without Science." In *The Notebooks of Leonardo da Vinci*, Edward Mac-Curdy, trans. and ed. (p. 910). New York: George Braziller.

Dawsey, Darrell. 2006. "Proof's Death Fits Old Pattern." *The Globe and Mail*, April 15. http://www.theglobeandmail.com/servlet/story/LAC .20060415.RAP15/TPStory/Entertainment (accessed April 15, 2006).

Doberman, John. 1997. *Darwin's Athletes: How Sport Has Damaged Black America and Preserved the Myth of Race.* Boston: Houghton Mifflin.

Durkheim, Émile. 1951 [1897]. *Suicide: A Study in Sociology,* G. Simpson, ed., J. Spaulding and G. Simpson, trans. New York: Free Press.

Dyson, Michael Eric. 2005. "The Culture of Hip-Hop." In Murray Forman and Mark Anthony Neal, eds. *That's the Joint! The Hip-Hop Studies Reader* (pp. 61–68). New York: Routledge.

_____. 2006. *Come Hell or High Water: Hurricane Katrina and the Color of Disaster.* New York: Basic Civitas Books.

Edel, Abraham. 1965. "Social Science and Value: A Study in Interrelations." In Irving Louis Horowitz, ed., *The New Sociology: Essays in Social Science and Social Theory in Honor of C. Wright Mills* (pp. 218–38). New York: Oxford University Press.

Einstein, Albert. 1954. *Ideas and Opinions,* Carl Seelig, ed., Sonja Bargmann, trans. New York: Crown.

Elran, Meir. 2006. *Khosen l'Eumi b'Yisrael: Hashpa'ot ha-Intifada ha-Shniya al ha-Khevra ha-Yisraelit.* [Hebrew: *National Resilience in Israel: The Influence of the Second* Intifada *on Israeli Society.*] Jaffee Center for Strategic Studies, University of Tel Aviv.

Emanuel, Kerry. 2005. "Increasing Destructiveness of Tropical Cyclones over the Past Thirty Years." *Nature* 436, 4: 686–88.

Energy Information Administration, U.S. Department of Energy. 2005. "Hurricane Impacts on the U.S. Oil and Natural Gas Markets." http://tonto.eia.doe.gov/oog/special/eia1_katrina.html (accessed June 1, 2006).

Entine, John. 2000. *Taboo: Why Black Athletes Dominate Sports and Why We Are Afraid to Talk About It.* New York: Public Affairs.

Everett-Green, Robert. 1999. "Puff Daddy: The Martha Stewart of Hip Hop." *The Globe and Mail*, September 4, C7.

"Facts about Lightning." 2006. *LEX18.com.* http://www.lex18.com/Global/ story.asp?S=1367554&nav=menu203_3 (accessed April 29, 2006).

"50 Cent Slams Kanye's 'Bush Is Racist' Comment." 2005. *Contactmusic.com,* November 1. http://contactmusic.com/new/xmlfeed.nsf/mndwebpages/ 50%20cent%20slams%20kanyes%20bush%20is%20racist%20comment (accessed May 23, 2006).

Forman, Murray. 2001. "It Ain't All about the Benjamins: Summit on Social Responsibility in the Hip-Hop Industry." *Journal of Popular Music Studies* 13: 117–23.

Frank, Thomas, and Matt Weiland, eds. 1997. *Commodify Your Dissent: Salvos from the Baffler.* New York: W.W. Norton.

Frankl, Viktor E. 1959. *Man's Search for Meaning: An Introduction to Logotherapy,* I. Lasch, trans. Boston: Beacon Press.

Freedman, Jonathan L. 2002. *Media Violence and Its Effect on Aggression: Assessing the Scientific Evidence.* Toronto: University of Toronto Press.

Freedom House. 2006. "Freedom in the World, 2006." http://www .freedomhouse.org/uploads/pdf/Charts2006.pdf (accessed July 1, 2006).

George, Nelson. 1999. *Hip Hop America.* New York: Penguin.

Goddard Institute for Space Studies. 2006. "Global Surface Air Temperature Anomaly (C) (Base: 1951–1980)." http://www.giss.nasa.gov/data/update/gistemp/graphs/Fig.A.txt (accessed April 24, 2006).

Government of Canada. 2002. "Study Released on Firearms in Canada." http://www.cfc-ccaf.gc.ca/media/news_releases/2002/survey-08202002_e.asp (accessed December 29, 2005).

Gracyk, Theodore. 2001. *I Wanna Be Me: Rock Music and the Politics of Identity.* Philadelphia: Temple University Press.

Gross, Michael L. 2003. "Fighting by Other Means in the Mideast: A Critical Analysis of Israel's Assassination Policy." *Political Studies* 51: 350–68.

Gurr, Ted Robert. 1970. *Why Men Rebel.* Princeton, NJ: Princeton University Press.

Hajdu, David. 2005. "Guns and Poses." *New York Times,* March 11. http://www.nytimes.com (accessed March 11, 2005).

Hamilton, Maxwell J., Elaine de Valle, and Frances Robles. 2005. "Damage Extensive Across Island." *Miami Herald,* July 10. http://www.latinamericanstudies.org/cuba/extensive.htm (accessed May 26, 2006).

Hamlin, Cynthia, and Robert J. Brym. 2006. "The Return of the Native: A Cultural and Social-Psychological Critique of Durkheim's *Suicide* Based on the Guarani-Kaiowá of Southwestern Brazil." *Sociological Theory* 24: 42–57.

Harding, David J., Cybelle Fox, and Jal D. Mehta. 2002. "Studying Rare Events through Qualitative Case Studies: Lessons from a Study of Rampage School Shootings." *Sociological Methods and Research* 31: 174–217.

Hirsch, Arnold R., and Joseph Logsdon. 1992. "Introduction to Part III." In Arnold R. Hirsch and Joseph Logsdon, eds., *Creole New Orleans: Race and Americanization* (pp. 189–200). Baton Rouge, LA: Louisiana State University Press.

Holland, Greg J., and Peter J. Webster. 2007. "Heightened Tropical Cyclone Activity in the North Atlantic: Natural Variability or Climate Trend?" *Philosophical Transactions of the Royal Society A* doi:10.1098/rsta.2007.2083. http://www.pubs.royalsoc.ac.uk/media/philtrans_a/Holland%20and%20Webster%201.pdf (accessed August 25, 2007).

Holmes, Tamara E. 2005. "Blacks Underrepresented in Legal Field: ABA Report Shows Stark Contrasts in the Career Tracks of Lawyers." *Black Enterprise,* August 2005. http://www.findarticles.com/p/articles/mi_m1365/is_1_36/ai_n15674277/pg_2 (accessed April 30, 2005).

House, J. D. 2005. "Change from Within the Corridors of Power: A Reflective Essay of a Sociologist in Government." *Canadian Journal of Sociology* 30: 281–314.

Huesmann, L. Rowell, Jessica Moise-Titus, Cheryl-Lynn Podolski, and Leonard D. Eron. 2003. "Longitudinal Relations between Children's Exposure to TV Violence and their Aggressive and Violent Behavior in Young Adulthood: 1977–1992." *Developmental Psychology* 39, 2: 201–21.

Hunter, Shireen T. 1998. *The Future of Islam and the West: Clash of Civilizations or Peaceful Coexistence?* New York: Praeger.

Huntington, Samuel P. 1996. *The Clash of Civilizations and the Remaking of the World Order.* New York: Simon and Schuster.

Ignatieff, Michael. 2005. "The Broken Contract." *New York Times Magazine,* September 25: 15–17.

Intergovernmental Panel on Climate Change. 2007. *Climate Change 2007: The Physical Science Basis. Contribution of Working Group I to the Fourth Assessment Report of the Intergovernmental Panel on Climate Change.* S. Solomon, D. Qin, M. Manning, Z. Chen, M. Marquis, K. B. Averyt, M. Tignor, and H. L. Miller, eds. Cambridge, UK: Cambridge University Press. http://ipcc-wg1.ucar.edu/wg1/Report/AR4WG1_Pub_FAQs.pdf (accessed August 25, 2007).

International Policy Institute for Counter-Terrorism. 2004. http://www.ict.org.il (accessed November 1, 2004).

Israeli Ministry of Foreign Affairs. 2004. "Palestinian Violence and Terrorism Since September 2000." http://www.mfa.gov.il/MFA/Terrorism-+Obstacle+to+Peace/Palestinian+terror+since+2000/Palestinian%20violence%20and%20terrorism%20since%20September (accessed November 1, 2004).

James, William. 1976. *The Varieties of Religious Experience: A Study in Human Nature.* New York: Collier Books.

Jervis, Rick. 2007. "Residents Return to New Orleans." *USA Today,* August 13: 3A.

"Jim Crow Laws: Louisiana." 2006. http://www.jimcrowhistory.org/scripts/ jimcrow/insidesouth.cgi?state=Louisiana (accessed May 29, 2006).

Johnson, Jeffrey G., Patricia Cohen, Elizabeth M. Smailes, Stephanie Kasen, and Judith S. Brook. 2002. "Television Viewing and Aggressive Behavior during Adolescence and Adulthood." *Science* 295, 5564: 2468–71.

Johnston, W. Robert. 2003. "Chronology of Terrorist Attacks in Israel, Part IV: 1993–2000." http://www.johnstonsarchive.net/terrorism/ terrisrael-4.html (October 25, 2004).

Karl, Thomas R., and Kevin E. Trenberth. 1999. "The Human Impact on Climate." *Scientific American* 281, 6: 100–105.

Katz, Bruce, Matt Fellowes, and Mia Mabanta. 2006. *Katrina Index: Tracking Variables of Post-Katrina Reconstruction.* Washington DC: The Brookings Institution. http://www.brookings.edu/metro/pubs/ 200604_KatrinaIndex.pdf (accessed April 24, 2006).

King, G., and R. Bendel. 1995. "A Statistical Model Estimating the Number of African-American Physicians in the United States." *Journal of the National Medical Association* 87, 4: 264–72.

Knutson, Thomas R., and Robert E. Tuleya. 2004. "Impact of CO_2-Induced Warming on Simulated Hurricane Intensity and Precipitation: Sensitivity to the Choice of Climate Model and Convective Parameterization." *Journal of Climate* 17: 3477–95.

Kolbert, Elizabeth. 2006. *Field Notes from a Catastrophe.* London: Bloomsbury.

Krupa, Michelle. 2006. "Presumed Missing." *Times-Picayune,* March 6. http://www.nola.com/news/t-p/frontpage/index.ssf?/base/news-5/ 1141545589263750.xml (accessed May 30, 2006).

Kubrin, Charis E., Tim Wadsworth, and Stephanie DiPietero. 2006. "Deindustrialization, Disadvantage and Suicide among Young Black Males." *Social Forces* 84: 1559–79.

Kurzweil, Ray. 1999. *The Age of Spiritual Machines: When Computers Exceed Human Intelligence.* New York: Viking Penguin.

Lapchick, Richard. 2004. *2004 Racial and Gender Report Card.* Orlando, FL: University of Central Florida. http://www.bus.ucf.edu/sport/ public/downloads/2004_Racial_Gender_Report_Card.pdf (accessed April 29, 2006).

Laqueur, Walter. 2004. *No End to War: Terrorism in the Twenty-First Century.* New York: Continuum.

Lenin, Vladimir I. 1964. "Book Review: N. A. Rubakin, *Among Books . . .*" In *Collected Works,* Vol. 20 of 45 (pp. 259–61). Moscow: Foreign Languages Publishing House.

Lenton, Rhonda L. 1989. "Homicide in Canada and the U.S.A." *Canadian Journal of Sociology* 14: 163–78.

Logan, John R. 2006. "The Impact of Katrina: Race and Class in Storm-Damaged Neighborhoods." Department of Sociology, Brown University. http://www.s4.brown.edu/Katrina/report.pdf (accessed April 24, 2006).

Logsdon, Joseph, and Caryn Cossé Bell. 1992. "The Americanization of Black New Orleans." In Arnold R. Hirsch and Joseph Logsdon, eds., *Creole New Orleans: Race and Americanization* (pp. 201–61). Baton Rouge, LA: Louisiana State University Press.

Lukes, Steven. 1973. *Émile Durkheim, His Life and Work: A Historical and Critical Study.* London: Penguin.

MacCallum, Gerald C., Jr. 1967. "Negative and Positive Freedom." *The Philosophical Review* 76: 312–34.

Mahoney, Jill, and Alan Freeman. 2005. "Rebuilt City Likely to Be a Lot Smaller—and Whiter." *The Globe and Mail*, September 17: A22.

Margalit, Avishai. 2003. "The Suicide Bombers." *New York Review of Books* 50: 1. http://www.nybooks.com/articles/15979 (accessed September 1, 2004).

Marshall, T. H. 1965. "Citizenship and Social Class." In T. H. Marshall, ed., *Class, Citizenship, and Social Development: Essays by T. H. Marshall* (pp. 71–134). Garden City, NY: Anchor.

Martin, Susan Taylor. 2005. "Can We Learn from Cuba's Lesson?" *St. Petersburg Times,* September 9. http://www.sptimes.com/2005/09/09/Worldandnation/Can_we_learn_from_Cub.shtml (accessed May 26, 2006).

Mattern, Mark. 1998. *Acting in Concert: Music, Community, and Political Action.* New Brunswick, NJ: Rutgers University Press.

McWhorter, John. 2005. *Winning the Race: Beyond the Crisis in Black America.* New York: Gotham Books.

Mead, George Herbert. 1934. *Mind, Self and Society.* Chicago: University of Chicago Press.

Mills, C. Wright. 1959. *The Sociological Imagination.* New York: Oxford University Press.

Mokdad, Ali H., James S. Marks, Donna F. Stroup, and Julie L. Gerberding. 2004. "Actual Causes of Death in the United States, 2000." *JAMA* 291, 10: 1238–45.

Moore, Barrington, Jr. 1967. *Social Origins of Dictatorship and Democracy: Lord and Peasant in the Making of the Modern World.* Boston: Beacon Press.

National Center for Education Statistics. 2004. "Table 303. Degrees Awarded by Degree-granting Institutions, by Control, Level of Degree, and State or Jurisdiction: 2002–03." http://nces.ed.gov/programs/digest/d04/tables/dt04_303.asp (accessed July 2, 2006).

_____. 2005. "Table 294. Earned Degrees in Economics, History, Political Science and Government, and Sociology Conferred by Degree-granting Institutions, by Level of Degree: Selected Years, 1949–50 to 2002–03." http://nces.ed.gov/programs/digest/d04/tables/dt04_294.asp (accessed July 2, 2006).

National Center for Injury Prevention and Control. 2006. "WISQARS Leading Causes of Death Reports, 1999–2003." http://webappa.cdc.gov/sasweb/ncipc/leadcaus10.html (accessed April 15, 2006).

National Rifle Association. 2005. "Guns, Gun Ownership, & RTC at All-Time Highs, Less 'Gun Control,' and Violent Crime at 30-Year Low." http://www.nraila.org/Issues/FactSheets/Read.aspx?ID=126 (accessed December 29, 2005).

National Weather Service. 2005. "The Saffir-Simpson Hurricane Scale." http://www.nhc.noaa.gov/aboutsshs.shtml (accessed June 2, 2006).

Neal, Mark Anthony. 1999. *What the Music Said: Black Popular Music and Black Public Culture.* New York: Routledge.

New York Times. 2000–2006. East Coast Final Edition.

Nordheimer, Jon. 2002. "Nothing's Easy for New Orleans Flood Control." *New York Times,* April 30: F1.

Oliver, Anne Marie, and Paul Steinberg. 2005. *The Road to Martyrs' Square: A Journey into the World of the Suicide Bomber.* Oxford, UK: Oxford University Press.

Oreskes, Naomi. 2004. "The Scientific Consensus on Climate Change." *Science* 306: 1686.

Pape, Robert A. 2005. *Dying to Win: The Strategic Logic of Suicide Terrorism.* New York: Random House.

Perina, Kaja. 2002. "Suicide Terrorism: Seeking Motives beyond Mental Illness." *Psychology Today* 35, 5: 15.

Picard, André. 2006. "The West Is Where the Heart Does Best." *The Globe and Mail,* July 5: A15.

Piven, Frances Fox, and Richard A. Cloward. 1977. *Poor People's Movements: Why They Succeed, How They Fail.* New York: Vintage.

_____ and _____. 1993. *Regulating the Poor: The Functions of Public Welfare,* updated edition. New York: Vintage.

Polanyi, Karl. 1957. *The Great Transformation: The Political and Economic Origins of Our Time.* Boston: Beacon Press.

Quaschning, Volker. 2003. "Development of Global Carbon Dioxide Emissions and Concentration in Atmosphere." http://www.volker-quaschning. de/datserv/CO2/index_e.html (accessed March 2, 2005).

Reuter, Christoph. 2004. *My Life is a Weapon: A Modern History of Suicide Bombing*, Helena Ragg-Kirkby, trans. Princeton, NJ: Princeton University Press.

Reuters News Agency. 2005. "Hurricane Dennis Killed 16 in Cuba—Castro." http://www.planetark.org/dailynewsstory.cfm/newsid/31634/ newsDate/13-Jul-2005/story.htm (accessed May 26, 2006).

Ricolfi, Luca. 2005. "Palestinians, 1981–2003." In Diego Gambetta, ed., *Making Sense of Suicide Missions* (pp. 77–129). Oxford, UK: Oxford University Press.

Samuels, David. 2004. "The Rap on Rap: The 'Black Music' that Isn't Either." In Murray Forman and Mark Anthony Neal, eds., *That's the Joint! The Hip-Hop Studies Reader* (pp. 147–53). New York: Routledge.

Schiermeier, Quirin. 2005a. "Hurricane Link to Climate Change is Hazy." *Nature* 437, 22: 461.

_____. 2005b. "Trouble Brews Over Contested Trend in Hurricanes." *Nature* 435, 23: 1008–09.

Schwartz, John. 2007. "One Billion Dollars Later, New Orleans Is Still at Risk." *New York Times*, August 17. http://www.nytimes.com (accessed August 17, 2007).

Sen, Amartya. 1990. "More than 100 Million Women Are Missing." *New York Review of Books*, December 20: 61–66.

_____. 2001. "Many Faces of Gender Inequality." *Frontline* 18: October 27–November 9. http://www.hinduonnet.com/fline/fl1822/ 18220040.htm (accessed April 20, 2005).

Sexton, Richard, and Randolph Delehanty. 1993. *New Orleans: Elegance and Decadence*. San Francisco: Chronicle Books.

Silverman, Adam L. 2002. "Just War, Jihad, and Terrorism: A Comparison of Western and Islamic Norms for the Use of Political Violence." *Journal of Church and State* 44, 1: 73–92.

Simmel, Georg. 1950. *The Sociology of Georg Simmel*, Kurt H. Wolff, trans. and ed. New York: Free Press.

Spalter-Roth, Roberta, William Erskine, Sylvia Polsiak, and Jamie Panzarella. 2005. *A National Survey of Seniors Majoring in Sociology*. Washington, DC: American Sociological Association. http://www.asanet.org/galleries/ default-file/B&B_first_report_final.pdf (accessed December 12, 2005).

Springhall, John. 1998. *Youth, Popular Culture and Moral Panics: Penny Gaffs to Gangsta-Rap, 1830–1996*. New York: Routledge.

Sprinzak, Ehud. 2000. "Rational Fanatics." *Foreign Policy* 120: 66–73.

Stephens, W. Richard, Jr. 1998. *Careers in Sociology.* New York: Allyn & Bacon. http://www.abacon.com/socsite/careers.html (accessed July 3, 2006).

Stern, Jessica. 2003. *Terror in the Name of God: Why Religious Militants Kill.* New York: Ecco/HarperCollins.

Strong, Nolan. 2006. "Lil Kim's Reality Show Scores Highest Debut in BET History." Allhiphop.com, March 14. http://www.allhiphop.com/hiphopnews/?ID=5460 (April 23, 2006).

Sullivan, Mercer L. 2002. "Exploring Layers: Extended Case Method as a Tool for Multilevel Analysis of School Violence." *Sociological Methods and Research* 31, 2: 255–85.

"Survey of Hurricane Katrina Evacuees." 2005. *Washington Post,* the Henry J. Kaiser Family Foundation, and the Harvard School of Public Health. http://www.washingtonpost.com/wp-srv/politics/polls/katrina_poll091605.pdf (accessed April 24, 2006).

Swidler, Ann. 1986. "Culture in Action: Symbols and Strategies." *American Sociological Review* 51: 273–86.

Taarnby, Michael. 2003. *Profiling Islamic Suicide Terrorists: A Research Report for the Danish Ministry of Justice.* Aarhus, Denmark: Centre for Cultural Research, University of Aarhus. http://www.jm.dk/image.asp?page=image&objno=71157 (accessed September 1, 2004).

Taylor, Charles L. 1985. "What's Wrong with Negative Liberty?" In *Philosophy and Human Sciences: Philosophical Papers 2* (pp. 211–29). Cambridge, UK: Cambridge University Press.

Tidwell, Mark. 2004. *Bayou Farewell: The Rich Life and Tragic Death of Louisiana's Cajun Coast.* New York: Vintage.

_____. 2005. "It's Time to Abandon New Orleans." *Winnipeg Free Press,* December 9: A15.

United Nations. 2004a. "Cuba: A Model in Hurricane Risk Management." http://www.un.org/News/Press/docs/2004/iha943.doc.htm (accessed May 26, 2006).

_____. 2004b. *Reducing Disaster Risk: A Challenge for Development.* New York. http://www.undp.org/bcpr/disred/documents/publications/rdr/english/rdr_english.pdf (accessed May 18, 2006).

_____. 2005. *Human Development Report 2005.* http://hdr.undp.org/reports/global/2005/ (accessed July 1, 2006).

_____. 2006. "Cartographic Section." http://www.un.org/Depts/Cartographic/english/index.htm (accessed May 2, 2006).

U.S. Census Bureau. 2002a. "Table 1. United States—Race and Hispanic Origin: 1790 to 1990." http://www.census.gov/population/documentation/twps0056/tab01.xls (accessed April 29, 2006).

_____. 2002b. "Table 3. Black or African American Population, by Age and Sex for the United States: 2000." http://www.census.gov/population/cen2000/phc-t08/tab03.xls (accessed April 29, 2006).

_____. 2005. "Hurricane Katrina Disaster Areas." http://ftp2.census.gov/geo/maps/special/HurKat/Katrina_Reference_v2.pdf (accessed May 30, 2006).

_____. 2006. "Entire Data Set." http://www.census.gov/popest/datasets.html (accessed April 15, 2006).

U.S. Department of Labor. 2004. *National Compensation Survey: Occupational Wages in the United States, July 2003 Supplementary Tables*. Washington, DC: Bureau of Labor Statistics. http://www.bls.gov/ncs/ocs/sp/ncbl0636.pdf (accessed July 3, 2006).

U.S. Geological Survey. 2006. "Earth Resources Observation and Science (EROS)." http://edc.usgs.gov/products/elevation/gtopo30/gtopo30.html (accessed April 23, 2006).

U.S. House of Representatives, Select Bipartisan Committee to Investigate the Preparation for and Response to Hurricane Katrina. 2005. *A Failure of Initiative: The Final Report of the Select Bipartisan Committee to Investigate the Preparation for and Response to Hurricane Katrina.* http://katrina.house.gov/ (accessed April 24, 2006).

Victor, Barbara. 2003. *Army of Roses: Inside the World of Palestinian Women Suicide Bombers*. New York: Rodale Press.

Wallerstein, Immanuel. 1974–1989. *The Modern World-System*, 3 vols. New York: Academic Press.

"Washing Away: Special Report from the *Times-Picayune*." 2002. June 23–27. http://www.nola.com/hurricane/?/washingaway/ (accessed June 1, 2006).

Weber, Max. 1946. "Class, Status, Party." In Hans Gerth and C. Wright Mills, trans. and eds., *From Max Weber: Essays in Sociology* (pp. 180–95). New York: Oxford University Press.

_____. 1947. *The Theory of Social and Economic Organization*, T. Parsons, ed., A. M. Henderson and T. Parsons, trans. New York: Free Press.

_____. 1964. "'Objectivity' in Social Science and Social Policy." In Edward A. Shils and Henry A. Finch, trans. and eds. *The Methodology of the Social Sciences* (pp. 49–112). New York: Free Press of Glencoe.

Webster, P. J., G. J. Holland, J. A. Curry, and H.-R. Chang. 2005. "Changes in Tropical Cyclone Number, Duration, and Intensity in a Warming Environment." *Science* 309: 1844–46.

Wilson, William Julius. 1987. *The Truly Disadvantaged: The Inner City, the Underclass, and Public Policy*. Chicago: University of Chicago Press.

Zogby, James J. 2002. *What Arabs Think: Values, Beliefs and Concerns*. Utica, NY: Zogby International/The Arab Thought Foundation.

Index